State of Vermont
Department of Libraries
Midstate Regional Library
RFD #4
Montpelier, Vt. 05602

SAVING AMERICA'S BIRDS

These Aleutian Canada geese are now considered endangered.

SAVING AMERICA'S BIRDS
Paula Hendrich

Lothrop, Lee & Shepard Books
New York

Photos on pages 2, 13, 48, 77, 79, 81, 84, 88, 91, 102, 119, 122, 136, 139, 140, 141, 142, 143, 144, 145 courtesy of U.S. Fish and Wildlife Service; pages 20, 129 by Luther C. Goldman, 46 by Wallace Bailey, 25, 67, 72 by Tom Smylie, 26 by M. C. Hammond, 41 by William H. Julian, 42 by John Wilbrecht, all courtesy of U.S. Fish and Wildlife Service; pages 8, 15, 124, 126, 127, 131, 132, 133, 134 courtesy of Dana Echols; pages 31, 33, 37, 38, 44, 63, 68 courtesy of Birgit LaFace; page 21 courtesy of Eleanor Nicholson; page 53 courtesy of Hawaiian Visitors Bureau; page 96 courtesy of John Borneman; page 107 courtesy of New Jersey Endangered & Nongame Species Project; page 149 courtesy of Atlantic Richfield Company; and pages 105 by Thomas C. Dunstan, 106 by Paul Lefebvre, all courtesy of AVM Instrument Company.

Permission to quote from Andrew Berger's *Hawaiian Birdlife* (Honolulu: University of Hawaii Press, 1972) has been granted by the University of Hawaii Press.

Copyright © 1982 by Paula Hendrich
All rights reserved. No part of this book may be reproduced or utilized in any form or by any means, electronic or mechanical, including photocopying, recording or by any information storage and retrieval system, without permission in writing from the Publisher. Inquiries should be addressed to Lothrop, Lee & Shepard Books, a division of William Morrow & Company, Inc., 105 Madison Avenue, New York, New York 10016. Printed in the United States of America. First Edition. 1 2 3 4 5 6 7 8 9 10

Library of Congress Cataloging in Publication Data
Hendrich, Paula.
Saving America's birds.

Bibliography: p.
Includes index.
Summary: Explains steps which are being taken to protect endangered species of birds in the United States.
1. Birds, Protection of—United States—Juvenile literature. [1. Birds—Protection. 2. Birds—United States] I. Title.
QL676.5.H38   333.95'8   81-15624
ISBN 0-688-00417-2   AACR2

Acknowledgments

EVEN A BIRD EXPERT, an authority on many aspects of ornithology and field study, could not write a book like this one without a lot of help from many people. The author is a bird lover, but not an expert, and she wishes to thank all the people who supplied her with much-needed information, helpful editing suggestions, and encouragement.

Special thanks go to Bev McIntosh, Tina Milburn, Dr. Tom Cade, Dr. Andrew Berger, Dr. Joel Pasco, Greg Hickman, Dr. Ralph Schreiber, Dr. Daniel Anderson, Dr. George Archibald, Joan Fordham, Ernie Kuyt, John Borneman, Dr. June Siva, Alice Berkner, and an added thanks to Richard Plunkett, who helped with editing of the entire manuscript.

CONTENTS

ONE	WHO CARES ABOUT AMERICA'S BIRDS?	9
TWO	WHO KILLED THE GREAT AUK AND THE PASSENGER PIGEON?	17
THREE	IT STARTED WITH GUY BRADLEY	23
FOUR	A DAY AT AN ANIMAL CARE CENTER	30
FIVE	THEY MEND WINGS AND RETRAIN BIRDS TO FLY	36
SIX	THE STRUGGLE TO SURVIVE—HAWAII'S BIRD PROBLEMS	50
SEVEN	A WONDERFUL BIRD IS THE PELICAN	61
EIGHT	RAPTORS—HANDLE WITH CARE	70
NINE	OF EGGS AND CHICKS AND DANCING WITH WHOOPERS	83
TEN	THE CALIFORNIA CONDOR—ARE WE ALREADY TOO LATE?	94
ELEVEN	WHAT WILL THEY TRY NEXT TO SAVE OUR BIRDS?	104
TWELVE	YOU DON'T HAVE TO BE A PRO TO BE AN EXPERT	112
THIRTEEN	THE GOOSE WITH A GREEN BANDAGE—THE STORY OF BIRD BANDING	121
FOURTEEN	WHERE CAN BIRDS GO TO GET AWAY FROM IT ALL?	135
FIFTEEN	THE CANARY IN THE COAL MINES	147
	FOR FURTHER READING	152
	INDEX	156

For this bird bander, climbing up to a nest of baby barn owls, bird protection is a risky business.

Chapter One
WHO CARES ABOUT AMERICA'S BIRDS?

BILLIONS OF BIRDS

IF YOU COULD go on some kind of magical flying trip back into time four hundred years ago, what might this country have looked like? Perhaps the first thing you would notice as you flew overhead would be hundreds of miles of deep forest, green and thick, so vast that not even the Native Americans would have seen some parts of those forests. The birds would have been there, however, billions and billions of them.

Leaving the forests, you would look down on the vast American prairies. Those prairies were sweeping grasslands then, not at all like the grain fields and farmlands now scattered across the Midwest. And you would see water, lots of it, for the prairies were once dotted with shallow, wetland areas called *sinkholes*. Where you saw water you would again see many birds, marsh birds and migratory travelers like Canada geese, blue-winged teal, cranes, herons, plovers, and sandpipers.

In that America of four hundred years ago there were no endangered birds. Many of the early explorers of the North American continent commented on the teeming populations of our wildlife, and they noted particularly the multitudes of birds of all kinds. Even seen in terms of the incredible changes that have happened to the land since that time, people still don't realize what these changes have meant for the animals and birds that were here long before we came. The earliest settlers on the American continent would never have understood that it might be important to save birds. Birds were there for the taking. People thought that if a bird wasn't useful it was probably harmful and should be shot. Back in 1630 in the Massachusetts Bay Colony it was common practice to pay bounties for dead eagles, and any bird big enough to shoot might have ended up in the cooking pot.

But today we can't take our birds for granted. Many people in America are working to save endangered birds. Many more are trying to save all birds from problems created by modern life. We have been a long time coming to the knowledge that birds need to be protected from people. Maybe we still need to be convinced.

Frightening Words from a Professor of Ecology

Every year more species of plants and animals are added to the extinct list, no matter how we try to stop the loss. According to E. O. Wilson, a Harvard University scientist, we may wipe out a million plant and animal species by the year 2000, if the present rate of extinction continues. If we ourselves manage to survive into the twenty-first century, we could be on a very lonely planet. While these are world statistics, the record here in America is no more encouraging.

Why Care About Birds, Anyway?

For centuries, people have been asking bird lovers why they care about birds. Who knows all the answers? Surely we care for birds because of their ability to soar and fly, their songs, even their beautiful feathers. In fact, the brilliant coloring in some birds' feathers gives us a clue about something that people and birds have in common: Both of us can see color, a quality many other animals do not have. Bird eggs have color, too, not often in Easter egg shades but still beautiful. Many people are fascinated with eggs, and a special branch of science, oology, is devoted to egg study.

Ornithologists are some of the people who care about birds. They are bird experts. (The study of birds is called *ornithology*.) If you asked an ornithologist why we should care about birds, you might get a puzzled expression first. Then answers like, "Because they are so fascinating. There's so much we still don't know," or, "Because they've been on this earth longer than we have, and maybe we can learn secrets of survival from them."

The Stupid Sea Gull

One thing even an ornithologist would admit: We don't care about most birds because of their reasoning abilities. A bird's two eyes will often weigh more than its entire brain. So when you call one of your friends a birdbrain, it really is an insult.

Sometimes how a bird behaves is an even better indicator that something is lacking. Watch the antics of a gull trying to crack open a crab by dropping it on the soft sand. The gull soars in the air, drops the crab, then lands nearby, looking puzzled as the crab crawls slowly away. The gull tries again and again, but it never seems to understand that the trick is to smash the crab on a hard, rocky surface so it can then gobble up the juicy insides.

Other birds use this clever technique very well, the crow and the raven, for instance. This brings us to an important question: When people call a bird dumb, doesn't it depend on what bird they are watching?

The Little Bird That Wouldn't

Ornithologists often find out about bird intelligence by accident. Professor Vance Tucker of Duke University was trying to find out how hard a bird must work to fly. He used two different species of birds for his experiments, laughing gulls and budgerigars (common parakeets). He put them in a test section with a wind tunnel. The cage was wired with a mild current of electricity, enough to keep the birds from landing on the cage, but not enough to hurt them. The gulls were easy to train. They soon flew whenever the professor wanted them to—but not the budgerigars. One little budgie grabbed onto anything that stuck out in the test area. When these perches were taken away, the bird still outsmarted the professor by hanging on the electric grid with only one foot. Thus, the electric circuit could not be completed and the bird couldn't get shocked. Another budgie proved it was almost as clever, using its feathers as insulation against shock. The budgie rolled over on its back on the floor and kept both feet in the air.

That "Disgusting" Creature, the American Vulture

Ornithologists have also learned not to make the mistake of thinking that just because the habits of some birds seem disgusting, that means the birds are stupid. Birds often have good reasons for what they do. Take our American vultures, including the condor. They have a habit of defecating on their feet and legs. Gross? No, not really. Vultures often live in hot, dry climates and their featherless legs get hotter than any other parts of their bodies. The birds' legs are cooled off by their own droppings and the drying process that follows. This gives them a kind of automatic cooling system that, although not as good as air-conditioning, works. Because of this habit of vultures, it would be foolish to place a bird band on any American vulture—wing tags, yes, but not bird bands. Their legs might become badly infected.

Mysterious Abilities of Birds

One thing all ornithologists would agree about is that birds don't think in the same way that people do. Much of a bird's learning has to do with *imprinting* and inherited behavior patterns. Imprinting means that, at times in a bird's development, a bird's brain takes in messages that stay with it permanently. These messages have to do with such things as the bird's ability to recognize its parents, and later its future mate, and to find its proper nest site. Thanks to the work of Konrad Lorenz, the famous Austrian ornithologist, we know that some ducks will even adopt people as their parents. If, just after hatching, they see a human being instead of another duck, their brain tells them, "This is your parent." That message never changes. It's an accident when this happens, but it does happen.

Ornithologists are learning more about such things all the time, but there is still much to learn. Maybe this is another reason why people care about birds. They have mysteries, and we always want to know the answer to a mystery.

No one has ever solved the secret of the long migratory flight patterns of birds, crisscrossing our world from one hemisphere to another. We do know that many birds migrate because they need to spend their lives in a summery climate. Some feed on insects and fruit that are available only in warm weather. Although we now know more about why birds migrate, the mystery is still in how they do it.

Recent research by ornithologists specializing in the study of migration shows that some birds take their bearings from the sun with incredible accuracy. Some even chart the night skies, the way

Flocks of birds like these migratory geese give us an idea of the masses of birds once so plentiful when this was a new and unexplored continent.

early human navigators once navigated the oceans. If birds have instincts like that, maybe they don't need our kind of intelligence.

As to the matter of a bird's eyes being larger than its brain, it may be that because of those instincts the important thing for a bird is to be able to see in a specialized way. Some birds see remarkably well at night and are aided by acute hearing. Other birds not only see color but they can see a far wider spectrum of color than the human eye can see. No one ever saw a bird use glasses or binoculars, but some birds—like the raptors, or birds of prey—see things at great distances. Each bird species has mysterious qualities that make it unique. If that species should disappear, its mystery would never be solved.

City Birds—Country Birds

Birds have made some remarkable adaptations to survive in some very unfavorable places. City bird watchers have seen peregrine falcons nesting and rearing their young on the edges of skyscrapers, feeding on pigeons from nearby parks. Recently, peregrines reared in captivity were placed on top of the Department of the Interior's office building in Washington, D.C. They seem to be thriving and have even produced young.

Every urbanized country in the world has its flocks of English sparrows, mynah birds, pigeons, doves, gulls—birds that get along very well with people. But what about the other birds, the ones that have become endangered or almost wiped out? *Habitat* is the word used to describe the places where a bird must live. Meadowlarks, marsh and shore birds, little grassland sparrows, all have different nesting and habitat needs than city birds. Slowly, the places where these birds must live are being taken away from them.

Problems for the Least Tern

One bird that has had trouble surviving because of habitat loss is the little least tern. These birds usually nest along the sandy beaches of both our eastern and western shores. Their population is very small on the West Coast now, probably because these terns can't find any undisturbed beaches where they can lay their eggs. The least terns of Florida, however, when they can't find beaches, have learned to nest on tar and gravel rooftops of commercial buildings.

Helen and Bill Dowling, a bird-watching husband-and-wife team living in Fort Pierce, Florida, once spotted two hundred pairs of these small terns nesting on the Sears, Roebuck store in their town. Concerned, they alerted the building's owners and the local Audubon Society. When the chicks began falling off the roof, Bill Dowling installed a four-inch-high railing around the edge of the roof. To prevent any further disasters, the Dowlings even trained some of the interested employees of the store in rescue methods for returning some of the hatchlings to their nests unharmed. The effort must

Here, a newly hatched least tern gets banded.

have been successful, because the least terns now come back to that same roof every year.

This kind of adaptation is what the bird experts call *marginal habitat*. Undisturbed beaches, rolling prairie lands, and virgin forests no longer exist in America. But unless we provide more than marginal habitats for our birds, we may lose many more of them.

A Bird in the Hand

There is a story sometimes told about a wise Indian, or an ancient Greek, or a sage Jewish elder. Today the story might be given a different twist with a woman becoming the main character. However the story is told, the point concerns all young people and what they plan to do with their future world. It goes like this:

A young man was jealous of the wisdom of the elder in his tribe, not because she was a woman, but because she seemed to know everything. It wasn't fair! Nobody had a right to be that smart all the time. Then one day the young man caught a wild bird. As he held the bird in his hands, he thought of the perfect trick to make a fool of the old woman in front of the tribe.

"I will go to that old windbag," he said to himself, "and make her tell me whether the bird is alive or dead. If she says the bird is alive, I will squeeze my hands together, then show everyone a dead bird. If she says the bird is dead, I will open up my hands and let the bird fly away."

So thinking, he presented himself to the old woman and posed his riddle. He waited, but she stood silent, gazing out into the open blue sky. Finally, the old woman looked down into the young man's eyes and answered, "The choice is yours, my son. The bird is in your hands."

Chapter Two
WHO KILLED THE GREAT AUK AND THE PASSENGER PIGEON?

THE AUK WAS NOT A MYTHICAL BEAST

ALTHOUGH THE GREAT AUK has been extinct for over one hundred years, we know what that incredible seabird looked like. Stuffed specimens are on display in museums like the American Museum of Natural History in New York City. We know that the great auk population was once plentiful, because residents of the New England coastline have given accounts of killing and trapping it, and the islands off Newfoundland and Iceland were once strewn with its bones. Who killed the great auk? What predators crept up on this naive bird who tried to defend its nest against giants ten times its size? The predator was man, and against such an enemy the great auk had no chance at all.

True, nature had played a sad trick on this bird. The great auk stood over two feet high, but it had wings too small to carry it into the air. This did not keep it from surviving, however, for like the penguin it swam the ocean vigorously, ranging from its nesting grounds off the coast of Newfoundland all the way south to the shores of New England. The great auk survived—that is, until people developed a taste for its flesh and eggs, and a market for its feathers as bedding stuffing.

Then the great auk's other flaw—if you can call it a flaw—came into play, for it would defend its nest no matter what happened. Although it couldn't fly, it certainly could have taken to the sea, swimming safely away. Instead, it stood its ground bravely but stupidly, apparently unaware of danger until too late. So the great auk was clubbed and shot and slaughtered by the thousands right on its nesting grounds.

A Final Murderous Act

In 1844, there was only one pair of great auks left in the entire world. A couple of sailors off their ship, harbored at Eldey Island in Iceland, crept up and clubbed them to death, smashing their single egg in the process. That act of egg smashing proved the sailors were not only cruel but very stupid, for eggs can be preserved indefinitely, and a great auk's egg would have become a rare prize. In 1912, a single such egg, preserved from a time before 1844, sold in London for 220 guineas, or approximately $660.

Those sailors did know, however, that the birds themselves were valuable. Museums had offered to pay large sums of money for specimens of this first rare, then endangered, and finally extinct bird. They got their specimens. Those last two birds ended up stuffed by a druggist in Reykjavik, Iceland, and sat in his shop window for all to see. A few eggs and even fewer great auks are still on display in their museum cases. The species is gone, but some feathers, bones, skins, and heads remain. The great auk stares blankly, its glassy eyes reminding us of the destructiveness of the human species. People destroyed this bird not deliberately, not because it was in any way a threat or even a nuisance, but because the bird was vulnerable.

Being Plentiful Is No Guarantee of Safety

Other birds have become extinct for similar reasons. Passenger pigeons once flew across America's skies in such masses they seemed almost to black out the sun. In 1813, the famous American bird illustrator John James Audubon observed a single flock of passenger pigeons that was over a mile wide and took three hours to pass overhead. According to the *Collier's Encyclopedia,* Audubon estimated there to be 1,115,136,000 pigeons. How could we possibly have slaughtered billions of birds in so short a time?

The answer is an ugly one, but it should be told again and again until the message is clear. First, Americans developed a taste for young pigeons—squab, they are called. People would buy as many as they could get in the city markets. Then the mass killings began.

People netted the pigeons on their nesting grounds and shot them out of the air. Because of the passenger pigeons' habit of massing in huge numbers to breed and nest, harvesting this "crop" was incredibly easy.

In addition, people were making problems for the passenger pigeon in another way. The natural habitat of this bird was among the vast forests east of the Mississippi River. These oak and hickory forests were being cut and cleared by the American pioneers as they pushed westward, changing forests into farmland. The loss of habitat may have been more critical to the extinction of the passenger pigeon than all the deliberate slaughter. But this does not excuse the behavior of those trappers.

THE POOR STOOL PIGEON

The cruelest method of trapping passenger pigeons was by the use of decoys. Pigeons were caught alive and their eyelids were sewn shut. Then they were tied to a perch called a "stool." When the trapper moved the stool, the pitiful birds flapped their wings as if they were landing on the well-baited ground. Pigeons flying overhead joined their ill-fated stool pigeon friends and were caught themselves. Sometimes a trapper could net over a thousand birds at one time this way. The passenger pigeons are gone, but we still have the term *stool pigeon* to remind us of this shameful practice.

There is another reminder, too. The last lone passenger pigeon lived in captivity for years at the Cincinnati Zoo. When it died, it was stuffed and placed on display in a glass cage. If you want to see it, visit the National Museum in Washington, D.C. Martha, as the bird was called, has been there since 1914.

THERE OUGHT TO BE A BETTER LAW

The wanton slaughtering of America's birds is not really a serious problem today, though loss of habitat certainly is. A new problem for birds and animals all over the world is now emerging, and it threatens extinction of several rare species. The rarer a bird or animal becomes, the more desirable it seems to be for certain illegal markets. Peregrine falcons, for instance, are endangered in the United States and rare almost everywhere. Recent news reports allege that a peregrine falcon is worth ten thousand dollars to some

Extinction is forever; passenger pigeons, like Martha, the world's last, will never fly again.

Arabian sheiks—not as food, of course, but for the sport of falconry.

To be fair, it should be noted that at least one Arabian country is using a much more scientific approach to its royal sport. Not only does the Emir of Bahrain, Sheikh Isa bin Sulman al-Khalifa, have his own personal falconer, but his son, Hamad, is supporting the work of an American ornithologist, Dr. Joseph Platt, a specialist in falcons. Dr. Platt has started the first breeding program of captive falcons in the Arabian countries. He also directs a $250,000 falcon center in the town of Zallaq with temperature-humidity-controlled chambers where breeding pairs can be seen through a one-way

This hooded falcon, on the eastern deserts of Saudi Arabia, is one of the hunting party of the Amir of Qatar.

mirror. This program seems a much more intelligent method of securing falcons than trading in the illegal market for peregrines.

THE HEROES VERSUS THE VILLAINS

Today's human predators may be more clever than the two sailors who clubbed the great auk into extinction, but they are no more heroic. Widespread news reports confirm that wildlife smuggling has become a major world scandal. It involves hundreds of millions of dollars, corrupt politicians, and even brutality to birds and other animals. One U.S. Department of Agriculture inspector, C. B. Williams, has said, "Right now there's as much money in smuggling birds as there is in narcotics." The heroes of this story are the people who track down these smugglers and who are working for stronger, more enforceable laws.

There is a United Nations treaty, signed by fifty-one nations, called the Convention on Endangered Species of Wild Flora and Fauna. Some countries honor this treaty, some do not. Recently the U.S. Justice Department set up a special task force to investigate this illegal trade. Agents patrol U.S. borders for smugglers and make arrests, but not enough to stop the traffic. The World Wildlife Fund is now raising money for something they call Traffic U.S.A. This group will check out the shipment of wildlife coming in and going out of American ports. All of these actions will help, but it is not going to be easy.

Remember: The illegal trade in rare species could, and probably will, result in the extinction of more birds. Transplanting a bird like one of the beautiful parrots of Central America to the United States seems harmless enough. But disease spreads rapidly through a shipment of improperly handled birds. Often they die simply as a result of human carelessness. In addition, very few of these birds, even if they survive, will ever become breeding pairs. Because of the prices they bring, however, rare and endangered birds are prime choices for this illegal traffic. The "Parrot Connection," as it is called, brings into this country such gorgeous birds as the hyacinth macaw for a smuggler's price of five thousand dollars.

The Dodo and the Calavaria

Before we allow another bird to become extinct, we might think about the dodo bird, extinct since 1681. Very few people would shed any tears over such a comical-looking bird, but the dodo did something interesting. It liked to eat the seeds of a tree called the calavaria. You'll find this tree on the island of Mauritius, where the dodo once lived. Three hundred years ago the tree, a valuable tropical hardwood, was found in plentiful supply. But by 1977 there were only thirteen of these trees left in the entire world. Why? Because to germinate, the thick seeds of the calavaria must go through the gizzard of the dodo, then be excreted or regurgitated. So, no more dodos, no more trees, despite the fact that the trees sometimes live to be over three hundred years old.

A final note shows how hard one ornithologist worked to bring a happy ending to this sad story of extinction. Dr. Stanley Temple of the University of Wisconsin is the person who pointed to the connection between the dodo and the calavaria. He even made trips all the way to Mauritius in order to try to save that tree. Just in time he successfully germinated calavaria seeds by force-feeding them to turkeys, whose gizzards (like the dodos') contain stones that do the necessary crushing. Although the dodo is gone, the calavaria has been saved.

Chapter Three
IT STARTED WITH GUY BRADLEY

A Dangerous Occupation

THE FIRST GAME WARDENS IN AMERICA were almost an endangered species themselves. They were shot at, threatened with physical violence, and, in one famous case, the first Audubon game warden in southern Florida, Guy Bradley, was actually shot and killed by an unknown poacher. The murderer—or murderers—went unpunished, but today that game warden is still remembered.

Several people may have known who killed Guy Bradley, and when his body washed ashore with bullet holes in it there was no doubt that murder had been committed. But that particular section of the Everglades was, and still is, a wild, isolated spot. Poaching was a way of life back in 1905, especially for people trying to survive in that swampy land. Some of the humans living there were probably as savage and bad-tempered as the rare Florida crocodile, which also made its home in the Everglades. What the poachers hunted for, mainly, was egret feathers. They tore the nuptial plumes from the bodies of the birds during the nesting season, and the birds were left to die.

An excellent account of all this is told by Roger Tory Peterson, probably the most famous ornithologist in America. According to Peterson, the poachers were so thorough in their job that they almost killed off the snowy egret species, as well as Guy Bradley. You may know what egret feathers were used for; they became an elegant decoration for women's hats. Guy Bradley gave his life to try to stop that traffic in egret plumes.

Many years later a marker put up in that area of Florida commemorated Guy Bradley's death. What would have pleased this brave man most is the fact that the poachers did not succeed in wiping out the snowy egret. Today those beautiful birds are plentiful again in the Everglades of Florida and seen in many other parts of the United States.

The People Who Follow Bradley's Lead

Guy Bradley would also be pleased to know how many men and women now devote their professional careers, and their lives, to the study and protection of birds. There are thousands of them in the country today, including the Fish and Game people working at state and national levels and people who staff special bird programs through private organizations like the Audubon Society or work in colleges and universities. It includes volunteers and professionals who run clinics for injured birds, and the over two thousand licensed bird banders in this country.

The heritage seems to pass from one generation to the next. Robert Porter Allen is dead now, but the work he did trying to save the whooping crane has been taken up by other ornithologists, like Ernie Kuyt (pronounced *kite*), Rod Drewien, and George Archibald. Charles Broley, "the Eagle Man of Florida," is also dead. Yet he would have been interested in hearing about the patient work of a young woman, Tina Milburn, who spent months watching over a pair of young bald eagles, trying to introduce them into the wild in an area where eagles had almost disappeared.

Rachel Carson is dead now, too, but many people have taken up her cry of warning about the buildup of poisons in a bird's body from the use of certain pesticides. We now know for certain about the deadly effects of DDT on such birds as ospreys, peregrine falcons, brown pelicans, and even some songbirds like the robin. It would be nice to think that in another generation or two game wardens and bird protectionists would be almost unnecessary. Of course, that isn't likely to happen.

A Problem with Hunters and Whoopers

A few hunters in this country are still remarkably careless about what birds they make their targets. Guns are allowed in all of our

Whooping cranes are not the only rare birds at Bosque del Apache. Here, refuge manager Dick Rigby (right) and his assistant, Gary Zahm, check the leg band on one of eighteen captive-bred, endangered Mexican ducks.

national forests, and hunting in season is even allowed in most of our wildlife refuges. However, no hunter has a license to take pot shots at anything that flies. In some areas game wardens must take extreme precautions to protect the really rare birds.

The Bosque Del Apache Wildlife Refuge in New Mexico is the winter home of a few endangered whooping cranes, and there is a sixteen-day hunting season for snow geese in this same area. How do they keep a whooping crane from getting shot accidentally? First, a few hunters are selected by lottery from the many who apply. Then, each hunter must pass a bird identification course. Once those hunt-

Some people consider the crow nothing put a pest, but that was not necessarily the reason for the trapping of these crows at the Lower Souris Refuge, North Dakota. Here they will be treated humanely.

ers know what a whooping crane looks like in the air, they won't forget it. Finally, hunters are issued portable radios tuned to a refuge station that instantly warns them when a whooper is on the way. Not one single whooper has been shot since this program started.

What If the Bird Is a Pest?

Another side to this story is that some people consider birds a nuisance to crops and property. There was a recent mysterious case of ten thousand blackbirds found dead in a farmer's field in upstate New York. At first it appeared that the blackbirds had foolishly eaten fertilizer pellets and poisoned themselves. The truth was they died from parathion poisoning. The farmer responsible has now paid his $1,250 fine for deliberately poisoning those birds.

There are other ways to handle such problems. Some farmers have learned to keep birds out of their orchards by broadcasting alarm calls that frighten birds away better than blasts from a shotgun. Spraying poisons to control birds can be damaging to crops and people—not a good idea at all.

The problem of birds around airports is a serious one, but it can be handled intelligently. The most critical times occur during take-off and landing because, obviously, birds don't fly as high as airplanes do. How do you make an airport unattractive to birds? Drain wet areas, cut down trees, change the ground cover to discourage nesting and feeding. Some airports even treat the soil to eliminate earthworms and use orange and yellow runway lights to discourage insects that are attracted to white light. Any hills and sand dunes not already flattened by bulldozers really don't belong around airports. The updrafts they create are too attractive to soaring birds like gulls.

It is astounding how persistent some birds can be, particularly during the mating-nesting season. In one case, during the hour and a half that a turboprop plane was idle on the ground, birds managed to build a nest in the engine intake. In Europe a group of jackdaws (crows) once hid seventy-two pieces of metal in a plane while it was inside the hangar. And one of those pieces was a small wrench!

Other techniques used at airports include radar detection, which is very useful to warn pilots of large flocks of birds, and recorded alarm calls, as effective for airports as for farmers. The Scottish Air Force has a unique way of controlling birds around its runways that some bird lovers might find objectionable. They use trained falcons as a kind of bird patrol, and it works very well.

A Big Bird with Some Bad Habits

Sometimes a bird that isn't really a pest can still be a nuisance. One place where people and birds aren't mixing too well is at the Naval Training Center near Lindbergh Field in California. A large flock of black-crowned night herons—more than seventy-five, at last count—has taken up residence there. These herons have been described as rather goofy-looking birds without the long, graceful necks of their more handsome cousins, the great blue herons. But ugly or beautiful, the real problem with them is that they are such big birds. They roost in the trees and have a habit of depositing droppings all over. Those droppings, by the way, are acidic enough to eat the paint right off a car. These herons have even violated the rules of Navy protocol by taking over the captain's fish pond. Perhaps someone ought to import those Scottish trained falcons for a military counterattack.

When is a bird nuisance not really a nuisance at all? When people are smart enough and determined enough to study that bird and discover everything they can about it. If those pesky black-crowned night herons persist at Lindbergh Field, they could be a fascinating subject for study. These birds in the proper setting—flying at sunset above the palm-fringed lagoons on the islands of Kauai—can be a magnificent sight. People could start asking these questions: Does this heron have any natural enemies or predators? Why do they want to roost in those particular trees? Are there any noises they can't stand? It is a fact that some sounds inaudible to the human ear can drive birds into a panic. Surely humans can show enough intelligence to handle problems like these without harming the birds. In these days when marginal habitats are often the only guarantee of a bird's continued existence, perhaps we should encourage the black-crowned night heron to go right on nesting there by the captain's fish pond.

Road Signs for Birds

There are plenty of people in that same general area of southern California who are willing to go out of their way to give birds a helping hand. In Newport Beach the light-footed clapper rail is now the first bird in the United States to have its own marked crosswalks. Three sets of warning signs have been set up on Back Bay Drive along the shores of the bay. This endangered bird, too, is anything but handsome. It walks with its head tilted forward in ungainly, high-stepping lurches. All it needs is a cigar sticking from the side of its beak to complete the picture of a Groucho Marx character—Captain Spaulding, perhaps. But the light-footed clapper rail has people who care about it anyway. The colony in Newport Bay is no more than 150 in number, but it is the largest light-footed clapper rail colony in the country.

In spite of the growing national interest in our country's birds, the truth is that we still don't know as much as we need to know about them. We especially need to know more about how they are adapting to our plowed-over, concrete-covered urbanized, freeway-tentacled world.

Bird Study, a Career Possibility—Or a Lifelong Passion

So many young people these days want to learn about birds that universities now offer courses and degrees in ornithology and in such related fields as bird ecology, wildlife technology, conservation technology, habitat management, and so on. Whether there will be enough jobs for all these trained people is another question. As long as the passion is there, many people will do the work—even without full-time pay.

Even before college some young people start learning how to care for birds. In chapter four you'll take a close look at such a training program. Nobody has yet established any Guy Bradley scholarships or internship programs for young people who want to study birds, but as long as we remember the efforts of people like Guy Bradley, the interest in protecting birds will surely continue.

Chapter Four
A DAY AT AN ANIMAL CARE CENTER

MIXING PEOPLE AND BIRDS—A VERY SUCCESSFUL PROGRAM

IN THE CITY of Anaheim, California, not very far from Disneyland, Greg Hickman operates his animal-care facility. A visit there is quite an experience. If you love owls you have come to the right place. There are barn owls, great horned owls, screech owls, babies and full-grown adults, each kind of owl in its own cage. Shifting from side to side on their perches, the owls blink their great yellow eyes. Sometimes, as if they resent being awakened, they hiss a warning, even at Greg Hickman or one of his young assistants.

Whether the owls know it or not, they are fortunate to be here. One, a great horned owl, came in with a badly damaged wing, a broken humerus. It has already made the trip into the completely equipped operating room for surgery performed by Greg himself. Hickman, though he has no degree in veterinary medicine, has had years of experience in animal care. "I grew up with animals," he says. "Been around them all my life."

HE WAS NO JUNGLE BOY, BUT HE KNOWS HIS ANIMALS

When Greg Hickman was only six or seven years old he began following after the well-known expert in exotic animals, Wesley Dickinson. "Wesley took me under his wing, you might say," Greg remarks without smiling. "He watched over me, saw how careful I was with his caged exotics—snakes mostly, but Wes took in anything that needed a home. And before long I was going with him to

This red-tailed hawk, one of the permanent residents at Greg Hickman's rehabilitation center, has been blinded by a shotgun blast and will never fly again.

help in his talks and presentations. We even did some motion picture work."

Then, after Greg was grown and working in zoo administration, he found that the North Orange Regional Occupation Center was looking for an animal-care instructor. "I thought of Wes," Greg said, "and realized I'd like the chance to help other young people who love animals and birds the way I do. They want to do something useful with their lives, and I think that's great."

Some Very Fortunate Students

There are eighty young people currently taking instruction at the animal-care facility. Some are as young as sixteen and are juniors in high school; others are in college, even doing graduate work. They will take three to four hundred hours of instruction before they leave. Some will go directly into animal-care jobs as veterinary aides or pet shop assistants. Some may go on to become veterinarians or take advanced degrees in studies having to do with birds or animals.

The laboratory is modern and fully equipped. Students under Hickman's careful supervision can do blood tests, stool samples, take cultures, X-rays, or anything else their bird patients might happen to need. In another room is an infant incubator currently being used by a pair of very hungry baby mockingbirds. "They're just about ready to fly out of here," Greg says. He taps on the glass and the hungry beggars' mouths immediately gape open for food. It's a warm, safe environment for these babies. If the incubator is needed for some other baby animal, the birds won't really mind. They will be ready for release in another week or two anyway.

The most advanced piece of equipment at the facility is a bone bank, a very fancy deep freeze for usable bones. These bones were donated by some of the more terribly injured birds brought in that didn't survive. The bones must be cleaned, sterilized, and exactly typed according to species and age of donor. Then, when some other bird comes in with a shattered wing or leg, it will be possible to do bone grafting right in Hickman's operating room. Hickman even does consulting work with veterinarians in the area who want to help with animal rescue work but have not had experience with this particular area of veterinary medicine.

What Is in That Box on the Doorstep?

The thing that Hickman is most proud of is that no animal or bird is ever turned away from his animal-care facility. "I never know what's going to be in some of those cardboard boxes people bring in," Greg says. "Sometimes no one even knows how the animal was injured. It would help if we knew how long they'd had the bird and what diet it was being fed. You wouldn't believe how many hawks are brought here, not just with injuries but with badly inflamed crops from being fed cheap, greasy hamburger for two weeks." Greg tries not to be impatient with human ignorance, but that's difficult for a man who has posted on his wall, for the benefit of his students, a sign: "*Rule 1*. The teacher is always right. *Rule 2*. If the teacher is wrong, refer to rule number one."

This pet baby roadrunner was brought in to Greg Hickman with hypoglycemia from an improper diet. It is recovering, and as soon as it is fully feathered it will be ready for release.

A Teacher Who Must Be Strict

Hickman is a teacher who demands discipline. "I'm gentle with animals but hard on my students," he says, "because if they don't do their jobs the animals and birds suffer." It is this attitude that makes it possible for Hickman to have such good relationships with the veterinarians in the area, the pet shop owners, and of course the California Fish and Game people who must supervise all such facilities.

At times, however, the stupidity and carelessness of some people are almost more than Hickman can take. "Sometimes," he says, "the ignorance is just criminal!" He points to a large male turkey that has been following him like a faithful dog around the outside penned area. The turkey is totally without breast feathers because of a temporary molt condition. The bird stops strutting as Greg scratches on its neck—if it were a cat it would be purring. "Somebody bought this gobbler as a child's pet," he says, shaking his head. "Apparently they didn't realize how big a turkey could get. When they ran out of places to keep it, they brought it in here." This kind of action is almost impossible for Greg, who has been around animals all his life, to understand. "It's incredible that people try to keep animals they know nothing about!" he explodes. "Can you imagine a full-grown owl stuffed inside a parakeet's cage? We had one here once, and how they even got the bird in there I'll never know."

An Injured Bird Can Be Worth a Thousand Words

Greg Hickman has little patience, either, with the extremists on the other side who think that all birds that cannot be released back into the wild should immediately be put to sleep—"euthanased," Greg calls it. Recently, he literally almost kicked a falconer out of his office. The man was hostile because Hickman has two permanent residents, a blind red-tailed hawk and a red-shouldered hawk whose wing had to be amputated at the second joint. The falconer thought the birds should have been "euthanased" long ago. "But we can't do that!" Greg says. "When a badly injured bird comes in and we know it can't be rehabilitated for release back into the wild, we can still use it for display, for educational work. It means a lot more to boys and girls who see such a maimed bird when you tell them, 'This is what happens when you shoot at something ignorantly or carelessly.' If they see the results of mistreatment and cruelty, it really makes an impression—more than all the words you can throw at them."

Those Illegal Birds Again

There is one other thing that rouses Hickman to near the boiling point: the illegal traffic in exotic animals, particularly birds. "It's the greatest source of our disease problem with caged birds," he says, "and it's almost impossible to stop this kind of thing. Most of the birds must be confiscated—if the smuggler is caught. And the sad truth is that when these crooks are caught and their birds are destroyed for being diseased, the smuggler just pays his fine. Then, because of some stupid legal technicality, it is even possible the crook will be paid for the confiscated birds!"

Life Is Never Boring for Greg Hickman

This is a busy time of the year around the North Orange Regional Occupation Center. It is spring, and often as many as eighteen birds a day come in. Nests may be uncovered by bulldozers, mother birds killed on the highways, and the season is just beginning.

Greg finds his work fascinating in spite of the frustrations and the lack of time for everything he would like to see done, at his facility and all over the state. He has a great interest in seeing wilderness areas preserved as refuges, but his time for this cause is naturally limited. Right now there are animals to be loaded into their cages for an all-day trip to one of the local grade schools.

"Have you thought about what animals we're going to take today?" Greg asks one of his college-age assistants. "It's cold outside, and I don't want any of my monkeys catching cold. We'll take the hawk, of course." Hickman nods toward a large outdoor pen where the blind red-tailed hawk sits, looking remarkably bright-eyed and intelligent. "That's probably the most photographed bird in the country," Hickman continues, "and the kids love her. I think maybe she likes the attention herself."

Just then the phone rings. Another interruption, and it's only a little after eight in the morning. Greg shakes his head, picks up the phone, then talks pleasantly into the mouthpiece. Just a normal day in the life of a bird protectionist.

Chapter Five
THEY MEND WINGS AND RETRAIN BIRDS TO FLY

SOME VERY SPECIAL PEOPLE

PEOPLE WHO RESCUE WILD BIRDS, badly injured by human contact, can now be found all over this country. It's too bad we need such people, but we are very lucky so many of them are willing to do this work. Whatever you may call them, they are not "little old ladies in tennis shoes." Picture Al Delgado on a motorcycle with a young golden eagle perched on his handlebars as he speeds through traffic out to an open field. There, Candice, the eagle, will have a chance to practice her flying, perhaps even to bring down a wild rabbit for food.

Imagine Toddy Powers trying to get a large Canada goose to spread its wings and take off for a return to the wild. Again and again Toddy leads the goose to an attractive wildlife setting. She turns to leave, but the goose is imprinted on her (it probably thinks Toddy is its mother). When she looks around, there is the goose waddling after her.

Try to picture Dr. Joel Pasco, veterinarian, with the pelican he befriended and nursed back to health. They go surfing together sometimes. The pelican, Rusty, clings to Dr. Pasco's shoulder, obviously enjoying the salt spray as much as any other California surfer. But there is a problem here, the problem of getting Rusty to go back to the sea on his own. It is another case of imprinting. Usually when the bird is mature enough and ready to mate the problem disappears, but not always.

People interested in rescue-rehabilitation of birds and who run

This adult pelican is not suffering from pesticide poisoning, but from human carelessness. Its feet are tangled in fishline, and it cannot swim or fly safely.

long-term wildlife facilities could tell many stories like these. Rosemary Collett, another well-known bird rehabilitation expert, has even written a book about her work. She sometimes has to swim out into the Gulf of Mexico to rescue badly injured pelicans. One such bird, made frantic by several fishhooks embedded in its flesh, stood its ground on a rock, fighting off all intruders until Rosemary finally captured it.

Protectionists can be found in many locations from the East Coast to the West Coast. Rosemary Collett's wildlife facility is in Venice, Florida. Toddy Powers works with her husband, Dick, in Norwood, New Jersey. Dr. Joel Pasco's Sun-Surf Animal Hospital is in Sunset Beach, California. This is in the same general area where you might see Al Delgado and his eagle, and where Greg Hickman operates his animal-care facility.

Dr. Pasco and Greg Hickman are friends. They share not only this common interest in injured birds, but both are members of an

Richard Knight (left), Dr. Pasco's assistant specializing in the care of injured wild birds, agrees with Dr. Pasco that this bird will live to fly and fish and swim again.

organization called AWARE (Alliance for Wildlife Rehabilitation and Education). This organization goes beyond just communicating ideas and sharing problems. It tries to unite the people doing animal rehabilitation work, setting up a network of cooperating individuals to be called upon in the case of sudden emergencies: oil spills, forest fires, or earthquakes. The organization is interesting, but the people who belong to it are even more interesting.

This Doctor Doesn't Talk to the Animals, But He Understands Them

You have seen what goes on at Greg Hickman's facility. Now let's take a look at Dr. Pasco's animal hospital. At first, this place seems like any other veterinarian's office, except that the beach is only a few steps away, and that the smell of sea air mixes strangely with the disinfectant odors. Then you begin to notice other differences. Rocking back and forth in a cage just above the pens for some ailing canaries is a baby barn owl. His stomach is now comfortably full, and he is about to settle down for an afternoon nap.

In one room you are invited to thumb through Dr. Pasco's scrapbook. It is full of pictures, stories, and snapshots of some past guests of this modern-day Dr. Dolittle. Besides Rusty, the pelican, and Stormy, a baby sea lion, there is Merlin, a great horned owl, and Spooky, a barn owl that bumped into a building and broke its beak. Marsha, a marsh hawk, is there, too. She came in more dead than alive after someone sprayed her with buckshot. After five separate operations she now looks healthy, but is a permanent resident with Dr. Pasco. Marsha will never fly again because there is a part of her wing that cannot be repaired.

One sea gull arrived only yesterday. Today, one of Dr. Pasco's aides, Kim Duncan, is carrying something in a soft towel. At first you think maybe it's a kitten or a puppy. Then you see the tail feathers sticking out and the injured beak. "I think God really meant this bird to live," Dr. Pasco says. "It got run over by four cars before the fellow who brought it in was able to reach it. And its only serious injury is that broken beak." How do you repair a bird's beak? With Elmer's glue, believe it or not. Later, the beak will be permanently coated with epoxy resin, the kind that sailors use to waterproof their boats. In the meantime, the bird has to be fed by a tube guided directly into its stomach and attached to a large syringelike plastic container full of a fishy-looking mess that is very nutritious.

Dr. Pasco combines two vital qualities that make him especially suited for rehabilitation work. First, he is a thoroughly trained veterinarian specializing in dogs, cats, birds, and small exotic pets. Funny to think of a birdman treating cats, but Joel doesn't find anything strange or funny about it. His pet black cat, Cedar, wanders in and out of the reception area, where a brightly colored pair of parrots squawk out fearlessly as if greeting an old friend. It's easy to see that Dr. Pasco loves all animals. This is the second thing that gives him an added dimension in his work with wildlife. Officers of California Fish and Game, who must supervise Dr. Pasco's work, give him high marks for his skill in treating a wild bird, giving it a good chance to survive on its own, and returning it as quickly as possible to its natural habitat.

In case you were wondering about Rusty, the pelican, Dr. Pasco says wistfully, "Rusty stayed with us until he was ready to leave, I guess. The last time he came back I fed him some fish up on the sun deck, but he soon flew off. Now, whenever I'm out surfing and some pelicans fly by, I call out Rusty's name. But so far none of them has ever answered back."

Dr. Pasco has such a special fondness for brown pelicans that he'd like to see AWARE, the wildlife alliance group he belongs to, adopt this bird as their symbol. "It was on the edge of extinction a few years ago," he says, "because of what we'd done by the use of DDT, which caused softening of its eggshells. Now it's making a comeback. People always describe the pelican as gawky and awkward, but in flight they look like a squadron of Blue Angel jets banking and peeling off, all in perfect order. Beautiful!"

THE SUNCOAST SEABIRD SANCTUARY—HARD TO SAY BUT FUN TO VISIT

Florida is another state that has many people committed to the belief that saving birds is worth all the time and trouble it takes. Two outstanding examples of this should be given here. Back in December 1971, Linda and Ralph Heath were out for a drive when they saw a cormorant struggling along with a broken wing. If you live in a seacoast area like Tampa Bay and you pay attention, sooner or later you're bound to discover some bird injured because of human carelessness. The Heaths didn't quite know what to do with the cormorant they found. They just knew they couldn't let it go without trying to do something. Now, a decade later, the Heaths operate their Suncoast Seabird Sanctuary, where they have treated thousands of similarly injured birds.

Ralph specializes in working with seabirds. Linda cares for land birds and birds of prey. She also raises the baby birds brought in during the nesting season. Of course, with so many birds coming in every day it isn't possible to manage things alone. The Heaths now have a number of teenaged volunteers helping out. Of all the birds that have been treated at Suncoast Seabird Sanctuary, Ralph Heath estimates that nearly 90 percent have injuries or ailments related to some kind of contact with humans.

This Canada goose at Blackwater National Wildlife Refuge has somehow gotten its neck entangled in a plastic six-pack holder.

Sometimes this is a purely accidental contact with monofilament fishing lines, or fishhooks, or the common occurrence of a bird getting one of those plastic six-pack carriers caught around its neck. The bird later hangs itself on a fence or tree, or starves to death because it can't swallow. But there are also destructive persons who are deliberately cruel to birds.

"Some nuts out there will do things like catching a bird, tying its beak together, and letting the bird slowly starve to death," Heath says. He has other examples of human cruelty, from speedboat operators who will deliberately run down a seabird, to the diabolical types who, knowing the pelican's habit of diving down on fish swimming in the ocean, fasten the fish to a wooden plank. The plank floats just below the water's surface, and when the pelican sights the fish and dives, it will often break its neck on the submerged board.

Ralph and Linda have not let such experiences make them bitter, however, for there are many concerned people who have supported

Litter left outdoors can often cause unforeseen harm. This ring-billed gull starved to death.

their work over the last ten years. The Heaths believe they have been able to save at least 58 percent of their bird patients during this time. What pleases them most is that now even healthy birds find their way into this haven. The Suncoast Seabird Sanctuary has become a refuge for all kinds of migratory and resident birds, who apparently know a good thing when they see it.

ALL THE SCHOOL CHILDREN KNOW ABOUT ROSEMARY COLLETT

Down the coast several miles, in Venice, Florida, is another place where injured seabirds have found a good home. Rosemary Collett and her husband, George, have founded the Felicidades Wildlife Foundation, Inc. Actually this is the Colletts' home and yard. They share their place with so many birds and animals that their daughter, Jan, must almost feel as if she has grown up on Mrs. Noah's Ark.

Rosemary shares her enthusiasm about caring for injured birds in many ways. She goes around to the many schools in the area and talks to children about her work. Usually she brings along a bird or animal—Barry, the barred owl; Snowflake, the crow; Lovey, the skunk—and she never minds if they steal the show.

The second part of Rosemary's work has to do with educating people on the hard job of bird care and rehabilitation. She has written a book on the subject that has so much helpful information in it that people who rescue and care for wild birds all over the country regard it as a kind of bible. Moreover, it gives a picture of the dedicated bird lover in action.

Those Hawk Lovers—Not Crazy, Just Dedicated

Perhaps the most fanatical of all these bird-loving people are those, like Al Delgado, who work trying to save injured raptors. The raptors are birds of prey, birds that hunt and kill other animals or feed on carrion. Some are night hunters like the owls, but most are daytime hunters, like the hawks, eagles, falcons, and vultures. All of them need special handling and long hours of patience to be rehabilitated. Maybe this is why raptor specialists are such a special breed of people. Many are young, a few are women, and all of them will risk personal injury to aid a raptor. If you've ever had a hawk's talon go clear through one of your fingers, you know that if you panic—try to jerk your hand away—you can end up with a badly mangled finger. Even worse, to the raptor specialist in this situation, is the fact that the bird could be further injured as well. So, you don't panic, you don't scream, you try to remove the talon as carefully as possible. Then you find first aid for yourself and the bird.

Actually, most people who handle raptors try to keep heavy leather gloves handy for protection as part of their standard gear. That's only one of the special kinds of equipment needed to care for injured raptors. There are special handling techniques that must be learned, too. One of these is a method called *hacking back*. This is a falconer's term for the job of teaching a bird how to hunt again on its own—to kill for food in the wild. Raptors, more than any other bird, cannot become dependent on humans and still sur-

Greg Hickman's young kestrel, soon to be released.

vive in the wild. If they approach strangers they are often killed, or they will starve.

No one is ever allowed to handle raptors without a special permit from the state Fish and Game office or licensing with the U.S. Fish and Wildlife Service. Lieutenant Brian Replogle of California Fish and Game says very clearly, "The only raptors we give rehabilitation permits for are red-tailed hawks and kestrels. In this state no one is ever given a hawk carelessly. We want someone who demonstrates medical knowledge of the bird's injuries, and someone willing to give unlimited hours to the hacking-back process—really an expert at this kind of thing. Rehabilitation permits are often for no longer than sixty or ninety days. At the end of that time, if the bird hasn't been rehabilitated, it may be turned over to someone else." If that sounds harsh and cruel, it isn't. The bird is what matters here, not the falconer's desire to train a hawk.

The Eagle Eyes of Texas

A few years ago, in 1976, Texas Governor Dolph Briscoe tried to make it legal for the ranchers in thirty-one of the state's counties to shoot down eagles. He did this because he and the ranchers believed the eagles were killing young calves, though most ornithologists would agree this is really unlikely, except in very rare cases.

Thanks mainly to the protests of one man and his supporters who helped him found the Raptor Preservation Fund, the governor lost his battle against the eagles. The man who stopped the governor was J. Shawn Ogburn. Later, his organization adopted a mascot, a magnificent-looking golden eagle, and named it Briscoe. Briscoe the eagle could not be set free because he was maimed in a hunting "accident" and cannot fly.

J. Shawn Ogburn is a young man who, like the Colletts and the Heaths, shares his home and property with birds. The difference is that all of Ogburn's birds are raptors. Since its founding, the Raptor Preservation Fund has helped to save over a thousand injured birds. Although Ogburn earns his living as a surgical supply salesman, his real passion is for injured raptors. And his wife, Linda, is an important part of the team. When Ogburn performs kitchen-table surgery on one of his patients, Linda, who happens to be an intensive-care nurse, will often assist in the operation. When the job is too difficult for these two to handle alone, they willingly turn the case over to a veterinarian friend, Dr. Bill Riddle. Dr. Riddle and Ogburn have pioneered delicate bone-grafting techniques that are helping to save injured birds all over the country.

There is one part of Ogburn's work of which he is particularly proud. He has a policy of turning permanently crippled raptors over to zoos. Then he persuades zoo officials to give him healthy zoo specimens (raptors) so he can rehabilitate them for return to the wild. Ogburn recently acquired a new sanctuary for his raptor recovery program. There is now a twelve-hundred-acre ranch in Texas that is not for cattle, but for hawks, eagles, owls, falcons, and vultures. "We put them back in the air," Ogburn says. "That's what my program is all about."

Bird Victims of Oil Spills

One of the problems that people in bird rescue work must face is that there are times when trouble seems to happen all at once—when there is an oil spill in the ocean, for instance, and hundreds of birds are washed ashore with their feathers so oily that they are unable to fly. In Northern California, at Berkeley, is a woman rec-

It was too late to save this oil-soaked common eider, found on Nauset Beach, Cape Cod, Massachusetts.

ognized as one who knows as much about oiled birds as anyone in the world. Her chief concern is in keeping them alive after they have been oiled so they can later take off on their own. Her name is Alice Berkner, executive director of the International Bird Rescue Research Center (IBRRC).

Alice greets visitors to that small building beside the Aquatic Park with her large dog in tow. Inside, the first thing you notice seems a familiar sight. Huge pictures of pelicans hang on the wall at the end of the room, below the beamed ceiling. It's a rustic, almost cabinlike interior, cozy and comfortable. Alice smiles as you stand looking at the pictures. "That's our Before and After set," she says. One picture shows the dismal sight of a pelican blackened and matted with oil. In the other picture the feathers are gleaming, the eyes bright and lively again. She would definitely agree with Joel Pasco—treating sick pelicans is only half the battle; the hard part is getting rid of them after recovery.

This place is not just an interesting setting for a woman who is indulging a pet hobby. This building is a research center, and the large aboveground swimming tanks beside the facility are an important part of it. They are full of aquatic birds, all recovering from various disasters, including oil slicks. When you ask Alice how she got involved in all this, she smiles again. "It was in 1971," she says. "Two oil tankers collided under the Golden Gate Bridge and spilled over a million gallons of fuel oil. A veterinarian friend of mine asked me if I'd like to help out. I thought, 'Why not? I can surely give a couple of weeks of my time.' Well, it's been a long two weeks."

Alice admits that at first she knew next to nothing about how to care for oiled birds, but at that time nobody else knew much about the subject either. It was largely a matter of trial and error, mostly error. There was almost no survival success back in the early seventies. Veterinarians, ornithologists, zoologists, and naturalists offered contradictory advice, most of it wrong. And the volunteers meant well but, sadly, they failed. No birds released after the Santa Barbara oil spill survived. Only 3 percent released following the San Francisco tanker collision survived. With most of these, it took nine months before a complete molt of new feathers made the birds seaworthy again.

Not Just Rub-a-Dub Ducky

After that first experience, Alice Berkner decided the time had come to start learning what to do, where to go, whom to ask for help. She began studying on her own and organizing for the future disaster relief of birds. It was a long process. Reports were contradictory and confusing. You should use solvents; they get the oil off better. No, solvents are dangerous to the birds and to the volunteers using the stuff. You should give the birds a cathartic to get rid of the ingested oil. No, you should not do this because it dehydrates the birds, and most of them are suffering already from a loss of water in their systems. Give them antibiotics. No, this makes them susceptible to fungal diseases.

The trials and errors went on and on. Any less determined person would have given up. But Alice Berkner is a cheerfully determined woman. She now has the cooperation of such diverse groups as the American Petroleum Institute, which has sponsored her work in the

These oil-soaked waterfowl were found washed ashore on the New England coast.

form of grants, and the U.S. Fish and Wildlife Service, which contacts her when they want to sponsor oiled-bird rehabilitation workshops throughout the country.

If you want to find out how birds are being cleaned these days, she hands you the booklet "Saving Oiled Birds," which gives a step-by-step outline of procedure. There is even a sheet of revised instructions telling how to make use of a Water-Pik tooth cleaner to scrub out those feathers.

"It's not just rub-a-dub ducky," Alice says. "Caring for oiled birds is a complex veterinary medical problem. Now we can save a lot of birds if we can get a team of experienced on-site workers there in time to set up rescue efforts. But there are still baffling problems that need to be solved, especially for some of the more difficult to treat birds."

SHE GOES WHERE THEY NEED HER

To the question, "Where was the last place you went to help out with a major oil spill?" Alice has a surprising answer. "It was in Wyoming," she says. "I know. I didn't believe it either when the call came through. But oil spills occur in inland waterways, too. This was on the North Platte River, and it was in April during the breeding season for a lot of birds in the area. A pipeline had broken and spilled oil along sixty-five miles of the river. We had mergansers, blue-winged teals, great blue herons, many more.

"The local Audubon Society had things set up as best they could when we got there. The first thing I did when I saw all those birds sitting on scattered straw was start hollering for them to get rid of it. It wasn't their fault. They didn't know that straw is the worst thing you can use for bedding because of the possibility of the birds' getting aspergillosis, a fungus infection. It's killed a lot of birds in situations like that."

Alice had good things to say about the cooperation of the oil company involved in this accident. "Their response was just outstanding," she says. "They helped out in any way possible."

Alice Berkner will go anywhere in the United States when called upon. "Technically, I'm still a volunteer," she says. Nevertheless, the research center costs close to twenty thousand dollars a year to operate. There is an office manager and one other staff member. The center does consulting work for industry, and Alice is a frequent speaker for conferences on the prevention and control of oil pollution, and for pollution-response workshops. Such events are sponsored both by the government and by the oil industry. They know that the work of the International Bird Rescue Research Center and the dedication of Alice Berkner and her staff have made oil spills a lot less disastrous for birds than they were just a few years ago. Not a comic-strip character, she's earned the title of "Bird Woman."

Chapter Six
THE STRUGGLE TO SURVIVE—HAWAII'S BIRD PROBLEMS

THOSE ENDANGERED BIRDS

NOW WE COME to the heart of bird preservation work. The people in the last two chapters were simply trying to save individual birds, restore them to health, and return them to their natural habitats. However, the most serious bird problem we face in America is trying to save birds that seem doomed either because their numbers are declining every year or because the population is so small that a single ecological disaster could wipe them out in one season.

Endangered bird programs are written about so often, are the subject of so many books, articles, and even much news coverage, that it's hard to imagine being able to say anything new on the subject. The situation changes almost daily. With human help, species that looked hopelessly endangered a few years ago now seem to be on the increase. But at the same time, other species suddenly drop alarmingly, and the reason must be found. There is even the case of a bird once thought to be totally extinct for over a hundred years, the white-winged guan, turning up in the dry forest areas of northwestern Peru fewer than twenty miles from the Pan American Highway.

The endangered bird list—which some senators would like to do away with—tells a story in itself. Here is one of the latest listings from the *Federal Register*. It is a complete listing for the United States, excluding U.S. territories like Puerto Rico:

The Struggle to Survive—Hawaii's Bird Problems

Akepa, Hawaiian (Honeycreeper)*
Akepa, Maui (Honeycreeper)*
Akialoa, Kauai (Honeycreeper)*
Akiapolaau (Honeycreeper)*
Albatross, Short-tailed
Bobwhite, Masked (Quail)
Condor, California
Coot, Hawaiian*
Crane, Mississippi Sandhill
Crane, Whooping
Creeper, Molokai (Kakawahie)*
Creeper, Oahu (Alauwahio)*
Crow, Hawaiian (Alala)*
Curlew, Eskimo
Duck, Hawaiian (Koloa)*
Duck, Laysan*
Falcon, American Peregrine
Falcon, Arctic Peregrine
Finch, Laysan (Honeycreeper)*
Finch, Nihoa (Honeycreeper)*
Gallinule, Hawaiian*
Goose, Aleutian Canada
Goose, Hawaiian (Nene)*
Hawk, Hawaiian (Io)*
Honeycreeper, Crested (Akohekohe)*

Kite, Everglade (Snail Kite)
Millerbird, Nihoa (Willow Warbler)*
Nukupuu (Honeycreeper)*
Oo, Kauai (OoAa) (Honeyeater)*
Ou (Honeycreeper)*
Palila (Honeycreeper)*
Parrot, Thick-billed
Parrotbill, Maui (Honeycreeper)*
Petrel, Hawaiian Dark-rumped*
Prairie Chicken, Attwater's Greater
Rail, California Clapper
Rail, Light-footed Clapper
Rail, Yuma Clapper
Sparrow, Cape Sable
Sparrow, Dusky Seaside
Sparrow, Santa Barbara Song
Stilt, Hawaiian*
Tern, California Least
Thrush, Large Kauai*
Thrush, Molokai (Olomau)*
Thrush, Small Kauai (Puaiohi)*
Warbler (Wood), Bachman's
Warbler (Wood), Kirtland's
Woodpecker, Ivory-billed
Woodpecker, Red-cockaded

*Note that all starred birds are from Hawaii.

What Does It Mean to Be on an Endangered List?

Being endangered means that experts have studied a bird and determined that the species is in danger of extinction through all or most of its range. The number may be extremely small, as in the case of the California condor, of which probably only twenty to thirty birds still exist. Or take the case of the ivory-billed woodpecker, so rare that no one is sure whether it even exists any more. The other woodpecker on the list, the red-cockaded woodpecker, might not seem so close to extinction, since it numbers close to a thousand. But it is gravely threatened by current logging practices in the southern forests where it makes its home. This woodpecker needs old trees that have died from something called red heart disease to use as nesting and roosting places. But now the trees are being cleared out instead of being left to stand. This is another example of habitat destruction, and in this case it could be fatal to the red-cockaded woodpecker.

The numbers of a few of the birds on the list have increased in the last few years, often because of extreme efforts to save them, although some drastic change in their habitat, some natural or man-made disaster, could still wipe them out. Some of these endangered species are in isolated spots where, if left alone, they might manage to survive on their own—that is, if their habitat is not destroyed. Those on the list with stars after their names all come from the islands of Hawaii. The danger of extinction to these birds —except possibly the nene—is one of the tragedies of modern Hawaiian life.

The Nene—A Comeback Bird

The nene, or Hawaiian goose, is interesting because an international effort has been made to save it. Peter Scott, son of the famous Antarctic explorer Robert Falcon Scott, is one of the best-known ornithologists in England. He established what we in America might call a captive-breeding station; in England it is called the Wildfowl Trust. There, the first scientific effort was begun to breed birds in captivity for eventual release back into the wild. In 1949 it became clear to the Hawaiian government that the nene was almost gone, and it agreed to let Scott do what he could to help save it. A Hawaiian rancher named Shipman had several pairs of nenes that he had raised on his ranch. Shipman gave some of his birds to the Hawaiian government to start its own captive-breeding program. Two birds, however, went all the way across the ocean to Slimbridge, England, where the Wildfowl Trust is located. Unfortunately, the birds turned out to be two females. The Hawaiians shipped over a gander as quickly as possible, and the breeding program finally started.

From those three birds, plus some wild nenes added later to increase the vigor of this captive flock, the Wildfowl Trust was able to produce a breeding stock of over two hundred birds. Many of those birds are back in Hawaii now, at the bird refuge in Haleakala Crater on Maui. Peter Scott proposed another idea for helping to bring back endangered birds: the "nene park" method, which is being used now at Haleakala National Park. A nene park is a closed acreage of land where several mated pairs are placed and left alone

These four nenes, a family of captive-bred Hawaiian geese, are of a species found nowhere in the world but Hawaii. The nene was once a water goose, but now lives high on the slopes of Mauna Loa, with only an occasional rain pool to splash in.

as much as possible. But they *are* fed, and their wings are clipped. After the young have hatched and left the nest, they are free to fly out of the fenced area, although they may come back to the protected area at night if they wish. They may even choose to breed their young inside the nene park. It's a case of being free to choose, and it offers more protection than just setting the birds loose to be on their own.

For a long time the Hawaiian Fish and Game people thought the nene parks would cost too much and might not be safe from predators. But the nenes are producing young, and now a similar park has been built on Hawaii in Volcanoes National Park. All of this points to a lesson about endangered birds that some Hawaiians now understand very well: Sometimes you can bring a bird back by captive breeding, but finding a safe habitat for that bird is not so easy.

Until the nene is truly abundant again in the wild, we can't say that it is no longer endangered.

What happened to those birds that Shipman gave to the Hawaiian government? That, too, is another interesting story about another interesting man. Ah Fat Lee was born in Hawaii. He once raised chickens, and almost all his life he has been interested in the science of *aviculture,* the breeding and raising of birds. Ah Fat Lee is now the chief aviculturist of a breeding farm at Pohakuloa, on the big island of Hawaii. He has never been to college, but he knows more about breeding birds than almost anyone in Hawaii. The Hawaiian division of Fish and Game chose wisely when they asked Ah Fat Lee to join the project to save the nene.

A man in his mid-sixties, he spends much time outdoors with those geese. Very few of his birds have been lost because of sickness. He keeps excellent records and is constantly trying to improve the breed by bringing in wild birds to mate with the captive population. If a mutant strain develops, Ah Fat Lee says that those birds must be eliminated. This is not cruel, just a very wise breeding practice.

At one time Ah Fat Lee had a breeding flock of some 30 pairs of fine Hawaiian geese, and Pohakuloa produced 100 to 125 goslings every year. For the 1979–1980 breeding season, however, the state cut this flock to only five pairs of nenes, probably because the federal funds for the program were about to run out. There is no chance that Ah Fat Lee will ever be able to set up anything like a nene park at Pohakuloa. The U.S. Army uses the area around the breeding farm for artillery practice—not a safe place for wild geese! Still, the number of nenes is increasing, and many of them are being successfully released at last.

Why Has Hawaii Lost So Many Birds?

Take another look at that list of fifty species of endangered birds; over half the birds listed are from Hawaii. Notice too how many are listed as honeycreepers. This is a whole group of related species, from the palila (dangerously close to extinction) to the amahiki, which is considered the "most common" native bird. Some of these birds have only Hawaiian names (and scientific classifications). Until you get used to the Hawaiian language, you might have trouble wrapping your tongue around names like: 'o'u, 'akiapola'au, nukupu'u, and akepa, even with those accent marks to help you. But whether you can pronounce them or not, you need to be concerned about them, for they may not be with us much longer. Even now, not many people have ever seen them.

On the Hawaiian islands, in a little over a hundred years, twenty-one bird species have become extinct, and even more species are now in danger of extinction. How did this happen? Island ecology is a very fragile thing. As people move in they bring pets and domesticated farm animals. They introduce plants, as well as certain diseases and parasites against which the native plants and animals have no resistance.

A classic example of this problem is the case of the Laysan duck. Laysan is a tiny island of one-and-a-half square miles, far out in the Pacific. It is now part of the Hawaiian Islands National Wildlife Refuge, but it was once the home of a family named Schlemmer. One member of that family, Tillie Laysan Schlemmer, was born on that tiny island shortly after her parents moved there in 1903. Tillie Schlemmer is now living in Honolulu, and she feels responsible—in a way—for what almost happened to the Laysan duck. She says that she wanted a pet, so her father bought some rabbits. That was not a good idea. By 1912, there were only seven Laysan ducks left on the island, because their habitat had been destroyed by the rabbits. Three species of birds on the island actually did become extinct: the Laysan millerbird, a rail, and a honeycreeper.

There is, however, a happy ending to this story. In 1923, a famous ornithologist, Alexander Wetmore, finally succeeded in having the rabbits exterminated. Today Laysan is the home of some six million birds—but no people. The Hawaiian Islands National Wildlife Refuge is one of the few wildlife refuges in our country that no one goes to visit except by special permission. It is a bird paradise, but for Hawaii's forest birds the story is somewhat different.

Hawaii's Birdman

Dr. Andrew J. Berger is another man to add to your list of interesting people who care about birds. Dr. Berger is a professor of biology at the University of Hawaii and has a long, distinguished record as a bird scientist. If you can get a copy of his book *Hawaiian Birdlife*, you will enjoy it. He first came to Hawaii in 1964 to be a Carnegie visiting professor for one semester. He went to India, studying and lecturing on birds there for nine months. Then he returned to Hawaii and now lives in Honolulu on the island of Oahu.

Dr. Berger is the leader of the Palila recovery team and a member of the Hawaii forest birds recovery team. Like most real bird scientists, Andrew Berger says he has been interested in birds for as long as he can remember. He is one of the few people who has actually held a palila's egg in his hands. He returned it to the nest, of course, and the female (perhaps sensing that no harm was intended) flew back to reclaim her egg. Later, he even took photographs of the newly hatched nestling, again without disturbing the bird, the nest, or the parents.

If you want to disturb Dr. Berger, however, just mention the fight that is currently going on between those who want to save the wild sheep for hunting purposes on the island of Hawaii and those who say that the sheep must go. These wild sheep are not native to Hawaii, but were introduced years ago, and they—along with some wild pigs—are destroying the native forests, causing the habitat of the palila, and the palila itself, to disappear. You can surely guess which side Dr. Berger is on. For years he has been concerned over the loss of those forests on the slopes of Mauna Kea, called the mamani-naio forests, for the two native trees that grow there.

Fortunately, Dr. Berger is not alone in his struggle to control the wild sheep and pigs on Mauna Kea. The National Audubon Society and the Sierra Club recently joined together to sue the state of Hawaii to make it get rid of those sheep. They are also concerned about the overpopulation of wild goats in Volcanoes National Park. This case illustrates how difficult the struggle is to save Hawaii's native island ecology.

Some Other Unwelcome Visitors

The main areas of the large islands of Hawaii—Kauai, Oahu, Maui, and Hawaii—have bad problems with what is happening to their native wildlife. Goats, sheep, pigs, cats, dogs, and rats—but no more rabbits—have all been brought into the islands from other places in the world. The mongoose is all over the islands (except Kauai). It was supposedly brought there to keep the rats out of the canefields, certainly not to kill snakes. There are no poisonous snakes on any of the islands. But the mongoose loves birds' eggs and has no natural predators to keep its numbers under control.

The pigs of Hawaii are a special problem, not only because they trample and destroy native habitat, but because no program of pig eradication has ever been supported on the islands. Many Hawaiians like to hunt pigs as sport and eat them at their celebration known as the luau. The pig is not a true native of Hawaii, though it has been there for a long time, in some cases since the Polynesians themselves came to Hawaii. Humans are the predators for the wild pig, and they are responsible for keeping it under control.

So many birds have been introduced to Hawaii that it is frustrating for the bird-watching visitor to try to spot native species. There are many birds to see—cattle egrets, mynahs, doves, house sparrows, house finches, mockingbirds, munias, red-crested cardinals, bulbuls, and various escaped cage birds—but none of these is native to Hawaii. Some introduced birds are multiplying so rapidly that they are probably causing a decline in the birds that are found nowhere else but on the Hawaiian Islands.

Efforts to set up captive-breeding programs on Hawaii have not been very successful, except in the case of the nene. The native forest birds, once safe in their lush tropical areas, have been reduced to small, isolated populations. There are bird recovery teams that study and learn as much as they can about these birds, which few people ever see, but Dr. Berger and his associates doubt that any dramatic method of saving them will be found in time. Refuge systems seem to be the only way, because the native bird habitat is so fragile.

But They Didn't Listen

Almost a hundred years ago, back in 1890, an English ornithologist named Scott Wilson became concerned about Hawaii's bird problems. At that time Hawaii was still called the Sandwich Islands and wasn't part of the United States. Wilson wrote of the dangers of cutting down Hawaiian forests and bringing in new bird species. "It would be a disgraceful thing," he said, "if such a Garden of Eden should be bereft of its birds. I am convinced these islands have a great future as a health resort for the inhabitants of San Francisco flying from its unhealthy and treacherous climate." He went on to predict "vast numbers of tourists flocking there and taking an intelligent interest in the avi-fauna [birds] of the islands." He begged landowners to unite and protect Hawaiian birds, to leave forest lands alone, and to *introduce no exotic birds.*

Well, the tourists came and they keep on coming. Some of them have even taken an "intelligent interest" in the birds on the islands. But many of the native forests are almost gone. As for the birds, Dr. Berger sadly reports in *Hawaiian Birdlife,* "There are some forests that at times appear to be completely devoid of bird life. I have walked through such forests, hearing only the sounds of my own footsteps. Upon stopping to listen, only two sounds reached my ears: water dripping from leaves to the ground or onto other leaves, and the monotonous call of a single species of insect."

Dr. Berger also explains that the first mistake the Hawaiians made when they cleared land was in planting exotic trees instead of reforesting with native plants. The reforesting was not a bad idea—it prevented runoff of water. But the interweaving of relationships between plants and animals was not considered at all.

In the 1960s native forests—and all the things living there—were further abused by defoliation experiments, chemical herbicide tests, military nerve-gas experiments, and bulldozing. As late as 1970, virgin ohia and tree fern ecosystems were bulldozed away. Dr. Berger is certain that, once lost, these native forest areas can never be recovered.

Let us hope it is not too late for the tiny Hawaiian creepers, the Maui parrotbill, the 'o'u, the palila, the crested honeycreeper, and others whose hold on existence depends on being left strictly alone in their unspoiled world. More trouble may be on the way to these islands, however. The United States has just banned use of DBCP (di-bromo-chloro-propane) in all states—except Hawaii. This is one of the nastiest of polychlorinated biphenyls, an industrial chemical that, like DDT, stays around for a long time. It injures not only wildlife, but is also a known cause of sterility and possible cancer in people. (There will be more about DDT in chapter eight.) As for DBCP, it is still being used in Hawaii to control pests in the pineapple fields. What the results will be if this chemical is mishandled is cause for concern, and the Environmental Protection Agency is watching things very closely.

Who Really Cares?

It would be wonderful to report that the entire country is now solidly supporting efforts to save endangered birds, but that is not the case. Some people think the whole thing is terribly funny, that it is just another case of some nice but nutty people gone crazy over birds. Some are even angry about it, and there is a movement afoot in Congress to repeal the Endangered Species Act.

Sometimes this angry attitude about birds is a result of conflicting values. Why wasn't the state of Hawaii concerned about the loss of the mamani-naio forests and the threat to the palila and other native birds in that area? Because that area on the slopes of Mauna Kea is also a game management area, a place for hunters to shoot wild game, including the feral sheep and pigs. The hunters were more interested in having something to shoot at than they were in the preservation of a few small and—to them—useless birds like the palila. The game management people had bulldozed the area and planted exotic plants that could be food for the game birds, but not native birds. In short, they were destroying the natural ecology and allowing those sheep and pigs to run wild.

This is an example of the wide difference of opinion that exists on the subject of bird protection. If you are interested in birds and want to try to save them, you have to take into consideration what other people want as well. The loss of native forests and native birds *is* important to Hawaii, important for the tourist trade, for instance. When all those glossy brochures were published by the National Park Service on "The Island of Hawaii," they spoke of reestablishing native ecosystems and protecting native biota. But no one can do that if the land is overrun with sheep, pigs, and goats.

A Final Word About Endangered Lists

Besides the endangered species listed here, some birds have been classified as "threatened." This means that, although not endangered, the species is likely to become endangered if some present trend continues. A threatened bird may not merit a special recovery program, but it deserves some careful watching.

There are also different kinds of endangerment: state, national, and global. Bird species endangered in certain areas may be almost plentiful in another part of the world. Take the Everglade kite, for instance. This bird is very rare in our country, but is still found abundantly in some places in South America. It would be bad to have the Everglade kite disappear from those swamplands in Florida, yet the species itself would still survive.

The Hawaiian birds, however, are truly globally endangered. If they disappear from Hawaii they will be gone forever, as will the California condor and Kirtland's warbler on the U.S. mainland. If we have to set up some kind of order of importance as to which ones should be given the most time, attention, and money, the globally endangered birds ought to come first.

Chapter Seven
A WONDERFUL BIRD IS THE PELICAN

A Funny Verse That Isn't True

> A wonderful bird is the pelican.
> His bill will hold more than his belican.
> > He can take in his beak
> > Food enough for a week—

So says the familiar verse by Dixon Lanier Merritt. It isn't true. The pelican *is* a wonderful bird, but it doesn't store food in its beak. A rhyming answer might go something like this:

> No pelican stores fish in his beak
> For an hour—or a day—or a week.
> > That pouch is a snood
> > For catching his food,
> Not for holding it there like some freak.

Actually, the pelican's beak is a remarkable adaptation of nature. With a pouch that expands to gigantic size underwater, it can hold two and a half gallons of water! This pouch acts like a dipper for scooping up fish. When the bird surfaces, it tilts its head down to let the water drain out, then lifts its head and swallows the fish—a very neat trick. Pelicans are strong, beautiful fliers. Remember Dr. Pasco's comments about the precision of their flight? And the white pelicans have another clever maneuver. Sometimes they cooperate in their fishing by forming semicircles of several pelicans and beating their wings violently as they skim over the water toward the shore. Then, when the fish are almost beached, they scoop up and feast on their catch.

What Pelican Are We Talking About?

Here is a good place to explain, to those who don't already know, about the different kinds of pelicans in America. White pelicans are not ocean birds. They live by lakes and other inland waters. They are gregarious; that means they stay together in groups and feed together. The white pelicans have never been endangered in the United States, except for the colony that nested at Great Salt Lake in Utah and was nearly wiped out by a crazy hunter who shot almost all of them with a .22 rifle.

The brown pelican is an ocean bird. It is divided into two subspecies: the eastern brown pelican of Florida, Texas, Louisiana, and the Carolinas; and the western brown pelican of southern California. Brown pelicans dive for their food. Sometimes, unlike their cooperative white pelican cousins, they even fight over fish and try to steal from one another. The white pelicans skim the surface to scoop up fish, but the brown pelicans are underwater scoopers.

The Troubles of the Brown Pelican

If these brown pelicans are so clever and so remarkable, why have they been having such a struggle to survive? The answer again seems to be because of people. The most deadly problem—the one that almost killed them off—had to do with pesticide poisoning. Several different chlorinated hydrocarbon pesticides have been used in this country since the late 1940s. Two of them have been particular problems for the brown pelican: Endrin and DDT (dichloro-diphenyl-trichloroethane).

At first DDT was universally regarded as a great blessing—the best bug killer in the world. But DDT doesn't break down into harmless compounds as some pesticides do. It stays around for years and gets into food chains. You may know all about food chains, but they are such an important part of this story that they should be mentioned here. Let's take an example directly related to the total loss of pelicans in Louisiana and the near-total loss of them in Texas.

First, the people of that southern area of the United States prac-

For untangling an adult pelican, four hands are better than two.

ticed massive spraying of Endrin and DDT in the 1950s and early 1960s. The pesticides were sprayed to control pests like the boll weevil, bollworm, and sugarcane borer. These chlorinated hydrocarbons washed into the soil and were eventually carried with the runoff after rains into the Gulf of Mexico. Then the fish began dying—not just a few, but by the thousands. Naturally, pelicans feeding on the contaminated fish began to suffer the effects of accumulated poison.

In the food chain, poisons like this become more and more concentrated as they are eaten by first one living thing and then another. The little fish are eaten by bigger fish, and the big fish are eaten by still bigger fish. Each time this happens the dosage of poison is growing, accumulating in larger and larger amounts. The Louisiana brown pelican, at the very end of this food chain, could not survive such an onslaught of poisoning. Every one of them died, and the people of Louisiana must have felt especially bad over this loss because it is their state bird. Today, the only brown pelicans in Louisiana have been brought in from Florida to help reestablish a breeding colony. Nobody knows yet whether these birds will be able to stay alive.

But Sometimes People Help

Another problem the brown pelican suffered at this time was eggshell thinning. Here, you should probably be reminded of something else: If people *caused* the problem of pesticide poisoning, it was also a group of dedicated, concerned people who found out what the trouble was and put a stop to it. Rachel Carson did not know about the problem of eggshell thinning and DDT; that came after her book *Silent Spring* was written. Dr. Daniel Anderson is one of those who helped prove the connection between thin eggshells and DDT. He is a professor at the University of California at Davis, teaching such classes as "Wildlife in Polluted Environments" and "Biology and Management of Wild Birds."

In his work, Dr. Anderson took the time and trouble to weigh and measure over three hundred clutches of brown pelican museum eggs. Some of these had been collected as long ago as 1879. What he was measuring was the thickness of the shells. (Museum eggs always have their insides removed before being displayed.) Up until 1946 the thickness of the shells was approximately the same, but by the late 1940s eggshell thickness was dropping. It continued to drop until after the use of DDT was finally banned in the United States. Then Dr. Anderson began examining fish (the kind that pelicans feed on) for evidence of chlorinated hydrocarbon residues. The connection was inescapable: The higher the concentration of pesticides in the fish, the thinner became the pelicans' eggshells. No doubt about it—DDT was reducing the pelican population by keeping their eggs from hatching.

Dr. Anderson worked primarily with the western brown pelicans of California, whose problems were almost critical at this time. They were contaminated by what he calls *point-source contamination*. A chemical company was actually dumping DDT wastes directly into the ocean close to where the pelicans fed. Some pelicans were dying outright from so much poisoning.

That Gunk on the Bottom of the Ocean

Another man who has very interesting things to say about brown pelican problems is Dr. Ralph Schreiber, curator of ornithology at Los Angeles County Museum of Natural History. He has given a very good account of the Endrin problem in Louisiana and has pointed out something else that we should all be concerned about: the contamination of mud in our ocean bottoms. DDT is not for sale any more in the United States, but it is still produced for shipment overseas! It was banned for use in the United States in 1969; however the dumping of DDT wastes into the ocean did not stop until 1972. Dr. Schreiber reminds us that though DDT breaks down into a compound called DDE, it is still poisonous. And it is lying on the ocean bottoms in polluted muds, waiting to cause the next ecological disaster. What will happen if these bottom muds are ever seriously disturbed, nobody knows. When there are major dredging operations in our harbors we must hope that gunk will stay down there where it belongs.

Looking Inside the Pelican's Nest

Dr. Schreiber, who met his wife when she was assisting him with his study of the nesting colonies of the eastern brown pelican, also makes very clear why eggshell thinning is disastrous for the pelican. The nesting bird grasps the egg in its webbed feet when incubating. A thin eggshell won't take that kind of treatment. Even if the shell is not broken, thin eggs often fail to hatch because there is moisture loss from inside the egg. The embryo becomes dehydrated and dies. And sometimes if the adults have too much DDT in their own bodies, they just stop producing eggs altogether.

Baby pelicans are utterly helpless creatures. Even at two weeks they look like some hairless, featherless, prehistoric, long-beaked, gray-skinned chicken. The only thing they can do is squawk to be fed. If you have ever seen pictures of a baby pelican feeding, you know that it sticks its head way down into the pouch. This may be where the idea came from that the pelican stores food in its beak. But the baby pelican feeds on regurgitated fish, not fresh-caught menhaden, pinfish, thread herring, or anchovies.

Bird Lovers Come in Pairs, Too

On the subject of people who help birds, here is something interesting. While even people like Roger Tory Peterson have said that more young men than young women have taken up the professional study of birds, what may have been ignored is the fact that many famous ornithologists have equally dedicated wives who share this interest with them. Sometimes both have degrees in ornithology, and in those cases they are truly regarded as a scientific team. Sometimes, however, only the husband will be listed in the scientific journals, yet he would be the first to admit that his work would not have been possible without his wife's help. This is certainly true of Dr. Ralph Schreiber.

He has described vividly what it is like to do fieldwork in the study of the brown pelican. He also says that Betty Anne Schreiber was there with him most of the time. They waded through mud up to their waists, trying to ignore such clinging nuisances as cobwebs, spiders, and even crabs. The baby pelicans sometimes regurgitated all over them or covered them with droppings as they tried to remove the chicks from the nests for weighing and examination.

The pelicans were never harmed by this experience, but it isn't a very dignified occupation for a doctor of science. Sometimes it's dangerous, as well, as when the twelve-foot tower that Dr. Schreiber constructed for pelican watching among the mangroves of Tarpon Key, Florida, collapsed. The accident sent him tumbling, in slow motion, into the mud below.

Only one other person was willing to help Dr. Schreiber day after day with such hazardous work. She wasn't even his wife at the time, but she is now. Betty Anne Schreiber is still helping her husband. Now it may be more a matter of typing and proofreading his scientific articles or assisting with other office and laboratory work, but no one ever truly understands a dedicated bird scientist except another bird lover.

A Final Word About DDT

Before leaving the subject of the eastern brown pelicans and Dr. Schreiber's work with them, we need to say one more thing about pesticides. When DDT pollution was at its worst, the pelican population was like a kind of barometer. As Dr. Schreiber says, "There is

This young brown pelican may have to survive many hazards, but at least DDT is no longer a problem for such birds.

no longer any doubt in the scientific community that DDT caused the pelicans' eggs not to hatch." He believes the brown pelican's success story should be told all over this country because it is one case of scientists' finding the cause of a decline in a bird species and managing to get something done about it. He adds, "Man might be wise to pay more heed to the pelican and other animals high on the food chain as sensitive indicators of ecological imbalance." If pelicans start to decline again, we'd better find out what the trouble is —and fast! For man, too, is at the end of a food chain.

There are still diehards—like the plant manager of Montrose Chemical Corporation, located in Torrance, California—who insist that DDT is "good stuff." "It saves lives," he says. And DDT is still being exported all over the world as a pesticide, especially to kill malarial mosquitoes. Montrose Chemical is one of the biggest producers of DDT in the world. What does the continued use of this

On Sunset Beach Dr. Joel Pasco releases the adult pelican that has been under his care for a fishhook injury.

pesticide mean to the world's ecological systems? We don't know the answer—not yet.

Recent Pelican Figures

According to latest counts, there are now thousands of eastern brown pelicans nesting along the coasts of Florida and the Carolinas. There are also thousands of western brown pelicans in the Gulf of California and the Baja area of Mexico. Colonies of brown pelicans that almost disappeared a few years ago from Anacapa and other of the Channel Islands in our Pacific waters are nesting again now. *Watch this bird,* not just for the pleasure it will give you as a bird watcher, and not only because it is one of America's comeback birds from DDT poisons, but because trouble for the brown pelican could mean trouble for people, too.

Chapter Eight
RAPTORS—HANDLE WITH CARE

Not Everybody Loves Them

REMEMBER HOW THE EARLIEST COLONISTS in this country once offered bounties for dead eagles, and how only a few years ago a state governor tried to introduce a similar bounty-hunting program in his state? It is true that there are people in this country who still loathe raptors and think of them as predatory pests that kill chickens, game birds, and even newborn lambs. To some weekend shooters, or "plinkers" as they are called, hawks, falcons, kestrels, eagles, owls, vultures—even condors if they can find them—are irresistible targets.

The argument still rages over whether hawks are good or bad as far as farmers are concerned. There is one incident of a young boy whose parents happened to be conservationists in a rural area, on a privately owned wildlife refuge in California. When the boy went to his regular Scout meeting he was horrified to hear his Scoutmaster giving instructions on the best ways to kill a hawk. These "varmints" were, as far as the boy's leader was concerned, nothing but worthless, harmful pests that should be destroyed.

The boy began asking some pointed questions. Did the leader have chickens? Yes. Had he ever tried to cover the tops of the pens with wire to keep the predators out? No. Didn't the man know that most hawks are actually good for keeping down such pests as gophers, field mice, and grasshoppers and that very few hawks are even big enough to carry off a chicken?

With that, the discussion came to an abrupt halt. The boy was ordered to leave the meeting for being disruptive and disrespectful and told not to return until he was ready to apologize.

An Ornithologist Who Cares

Compare that Scout leader's attitude with the work of one of our country's leading ornithologists, Dr. Joseph J. Hickey. Over ten years ago Hickey became concerned about what was happening to peregrine falcons in this country. In the late 1960s peregrines, too, were suffering the terrible effects of DDT poisoning, though no one knew exactly what the trouble was at the time. Dr. Hickey, who was teaching at the University of Wisconsin in Madison, suspected that there was something wrong with the peregrines.

With the aid of one of his graduate students, Hickey arranged a survey of all the known peregrine *aeries,* or nesting spots, east of the Mississippi River that had been noted in ornithological records. This was no easy task, for aeries are usually high up on some craggy rock or other inaccessible spot. However, that survey resulted in an incredible discovery: In all the land east of the Mississippi River there were *no breeding peregrine falcons!* We had already lost them as a breeding species in the East and didn't even know it.

It was this discovery that alerted us to the fact that there was something drastically wrong in the environment. Birds are sensitive monitors of ecological imbalance, and the peregrine falcon is at the top of a long and complicated food chain. It was later found that the same thing was occurring with the bald eagle and the brown pelican. Dr. Hickey's survey was taken several years before the discovery, in Great Britain, of the phenomenon of eggshell thinning. Thus the peregrine actually served as an early warning system telling us of an ecological disaster.

Sometimes Hating Raptors Can Be a Sickness

There are still people who would say, "So what? Who needs a peregrine falcon, or any raptor for that matter?" A few individuals have such a dislike of raptors that it cannot be called anything but a sickness. Here is a gruesome example that concerns the first early attempts to breed peregrine falcons in captivity (because their eggs weren't hatching).

The most famous of these "peregrine hatcheries" is at Cornell

This adult peregrine falcon is old enough to mate and rear its young. Only a few years ago eggshell thinning made raising young peregrines almost impossible.

University Laboratory of Ornithology in Ithaca, New York. The first ornithologist in America to breed the peregrine falcon in captivity was Heinz Meng, a biology professor at the State University of New York at New Paltz. He lent to Dr. Tom Cade, and the Cornell Laboratory, the first breeding pair. In gratitude for this gift, Dr. Cade, in the summer of 1974, gave to Meng the first pair of Cornell-raised peregrines. They were to be used for a release experiment on the New Paltz campus.

Newspaper reports came out about Meng's planned release of these birds from a building called the faculty tower. Then Meng began to get threatening phone calls: Something was going to happen to the birds. Only a short time later, Meng found the female mutilated. One wing, cut off from her body with a sharp instrument, was found half a mile away from the faculty tower. A week later, the male disappeared without a trace. No one was ever arrested, but these sad acts couldn't have been accidents.

A couple of years later, in 1976, a planned release of peregrines in western Massachusetts brought an outcry of protest from local newspapers. Hawk haters began writing letters about these "killer birds" soon to be released to prey upon innocent songbirds and the hunters' own favorite target, ducks. To be fair, peregrines will eat ducks.

The common name of this species used to be "duck hawks." But peregrine falcons have never been a serious threat to duck populations. They kill far fewer of them than hunters do.

One other famous case occurred in Wyoming, where fifty golden eagles were illegally slaughtered. Haunches of illegally killed pronghorn antelope had been laced with poison and scattered on the rough, rocky ground—a feast too tempting for the eagles to pass up. After a public outcry of this wanton killing forced an investigation, an employee of the cooperative federal-state predator program was convicted. However, his conviction was *not* for killing eagles. It was for shooting pronghorns out of season!

Public opinion does seem to be changing as far as raptors are concerned. A graduate student from Cornell, John Wiessinger, recently took a poll in Atlantic County, New Jersey, to find out how people felt about the planned release of peregrines at the Brigantine National Wildlife Refuge. Audubon Society members favored release by 75 percent; visitors to the wildlife refuge favored the plan by 76 percent; and even those from the general community were 63 percent in favor of the idea. Oddly, but interestingly, 92 percent of the hunters questioned favored reintroduction of the peregrines to the refuge where ducks are plentiful. Maybe this is because real hunters are often well informed about the ecological need for predators in keeping a balance of nature.

There is a problem with the shooting of newly released young peregrines, but this is not usually done by experienced hunters. The real problem is casual target practice by those "plinkers" with guns who will shoot at anything that flies—especially a soaring raptor.

If You Don't Hate Them, You May Learn to Love Them

For all the hawk, eagle, and falcon haters in this country, there must be many more, the falconers for example, who really love these birds. Many highly trained ornithologists started out as falconers. The most well-known raptor man in the country, Dr. Tom Cade, the founder-director of the peregrine breeding project at Cornell, takes an interesting position regarding falconry.

Dr. Cade believes falconry is a legitimate and justifiable field sport, if people are willing to obey the federal and state laws concerning it. He thinks young people must understand that it is a demanding sport requiring a lot of technical skill, years of dedicated effort, and a willingness to learn about the habits of raptors and their prey. This last, he says, may actually lead to scientific nature study. Here he cites the famous case of Frederick II, a medieval king of Germany, who wrote the first real book of ornithology because of his studies as a falconer.

Tom Cade understands the thrill of falconry very well. He knows what it is like to release a bird into the air, watch it soar free into the blue sky with those sharp-pointed wings, then dive suddenly, for the first time, on its own natural prey. "In the final analysis," Tom Cade says, "I guess falconry really is just a specialized form of birdwatching, which is also a sport."

More Pros and Cons of Falconry

As Dr. Cade makes very clear, falconry is never easy. There is a big difference between a falconer and the casual owner of a pet bird. Falconers know they are dealing with a wild animal, not a tame one. That hawk or eagle still longs to be free. It may actually regard its trainer with feelings that humans would call fear, distrust, even hatred.

But suppose a bond does develop between the falcon and the falconer. Real falconers must always face the day when they feel honor-bound to start the hacking-back process to let the bird go free again. They may have learned a lot about the behavior of raptors during this time, and if the bird successfully returns to its free state nothing will have been lost. Often, however, the story can have a sad ending. The bird, grown used to human contact, approaches a stranger fearlessly and is shot.

For this reason, the hacking back to the wild, the breaking of that human bond, is the most important thing a falconer can learn. The bird must not be dependent on people for food. On this subject the "Peregrine Fund Newsletter" says, "The best way to judge the individual fitness of a falcon for survival is how well it performs as a hunter." That is what nature has molded and selected the bird for, and everything that makes it a falcon is related to this ability to catch prey.

You won't be allowed to train a peregrine, anyway, even if you can find one. In most states, to keep even a hawk or a kestrel you must have a falconer's license. The rules are very strict and are spelled out in many pages of regulations. Not many parents are willing to take on this kind of responsibility for a hawk-crazy son or daughter. One woman with a son and a husband who are both avid falconers explained it this way:

> Did you know that hawks eat nearly two pounds of meat every day, even the baby ones? That's cut-up beef heart fresh from the store; it has to be bloody. Besides that, my son usually kills one sparrow every day, or some other nuisance bird like the starling, and feeds it to his hawk whole—feathers, claws, and all. I don't think the neighbors understand, but that's what he says has to be done. This helpless little baby—three pounds of feathers, claws, and screeches—Do you know where we had to keep it when it was first given to us? In our bathroom, that's where. My window drapes and shower curtains were in shreds before they finally got the hawk house built in the backyard. And good heavens! The mess!

If you are determined to become a falconer, try always to think of it as Tom Cade thinks of it: a serious learning experience only for the most dedicated of aspiring ornithologists. Then perhaps someday you may get a chance to visit the breeding lofts at Cornell, or one of the three twelve-unit breeding lofts at Fort Collins, Colorado, where much of the captive breeding of peregrines takes place in this country.

These "Barns" Are Not for Farm Animals

In 1970, Dr. Tom Cade founded his Peregrine Fund and began his long-term program of research at Cornell University. He and his researchers wanted to breed peregrines in captivity, with the idea that the chicks produced and raised there would help increase wild populations later on. At first, there was not much support for Dr. Cade's idea. It was regarded as unproven and even controversial. Then, later, the Audubon Society came forward with forty thousand dollars to help build the first and second of the twelve-unit breeding lofts at Fort Collins, Colorado. This was a real boost to the peregrine program, for at last people began to pay attention to the work going on both at Cornell and Fort Collins.

Those breeding lofts may look from the outside like large barns to some people, but some rather strange and interesting things go on inside. Results have often been surprisingly good. The number of young peregrines produced has been gradually increasing each year.

Many eggs are incubated in a special air-and-humidity-controlled incubator lab. The females have been stimulated to lay again and again by removing their eggs each time they lay. For example, at Cornell in 1979 21 females laid a total of 127 eggs. Only 107 of these eggs were actually fertile. Seventy-one eggs hatched (more probably would have hatched, but they had just been moved into a new incubator lab and the new equipment needed some adjustment). Of those 71 hatchlings, 57 survived to full development.

Some of the male and female pairs mate normally at Cornell, after they are properly matched up. In one case, a very aggressive and dominant male was tried with six different females before the Cornell matchmakers had success. The mate finally chosen was rather small and quiet, but she responded well to the aggressive male, and now they have become a most productive pair.

Some male peregrine falcons are allowed deliberately to become imprinted on the people who handle them. In fact, they actually become sexually responsive to their handlers, but not to the female peregrines. It is from these birds that the people at Cornell get the sperm for artificial insemination. Similarly, the females who imprint on people must be inseminated to produce fertile eggs.

You may know that sperm are the reproductive cells that come from the male bird, and when implanted into the female's cloaca during mating these sperm fertilize the eggs that will eventually produce a new bird. What you may not know is that aviculturists and ornithologists have now perfected techniques for implanting the male sperm into the female and fertilizing her eggs without the male bird even being present. This is called *artificial insemination*, a valuable tool for preserving endangered birds, but it may not be possible for use with all endangered birds. Scientists still have much to learn about the complex breeding cycles of different species.

The Peregrine Fund has expanded its facilities in recent years. It now includes a residence-office-laboratory complex at Fort Collins, with a new pole barn located nearby. There are two private cooperative facilities, one in Wyoming and one in New Mexico. Much of this expansion became possible because of private donations, totaling over ninety thousand dollars just in 1979.

Its wings spread for take-off, this falcon finds safe refuge at Yukon Flats Monument.

It is possible for visitors to go inside the falcon lofts at Cornell, although by appointment only. There is no visitation during the breeding season, from February 1 to August 15. They might very well hang a sign on the door: FALCONS BREEDING—DO NOT DISTURB.

But How Do They Get Them Back into the Wild?

Each year since 1974, when the Peregrine Fund first began releasing captive-bred peregrines, the number of birds successfully released into the wild has climbed steadily. Some have been released into wildlife refuges, with whole teams of field-workers watching over them. There have been more than a hundred of these young men and women, mostly college students, working summer after summer. Young hatchlings have been put into nests of wild peregrine adults whose eggs didn't hatch, or sometimes they are put into prairie falcon nests.

It's a hard job watching over these chicks. They have to be guarded carefully against the predations of great horned owls and golden eagles. In addition, in the first free flights from the release site there is no way to prevent the young peregrines from flying too far away and never returning. However, the work can be satisfying, too, especially when you know you have succeeded.

The release of peregrine falcons into urban sites has been much publicized, and remarkably successful in some cases. The recent releases in Washington, Baltimore, and New York City were not just publicity stunts. Cities actually offer a very good habitat for falcons, as the peregrines themselves discovered in the late 1930s and early 1940s (before DDT severely affected their population in the East). Skyscrapers serve as artificial cliffs, and the updrafts of wind against those "concrete canyons" help lift the birds into the air. There are no hunters in cities. Even more important, there is plenty of food in the form of pigeons, starlings, and sparrows, and there are *no owls* on those tall buildings to prey upon the defenseless young peregrines.

Paradise for Raptors

If you prefer to think of raptors in a wilderness setting, there is good news here, too. On the Snake River in Idaho is a place called the Birds of Prey Natural Area. It has the densest population of raptors in the world. Golden eagles perch on craggy rocks that no human can reach. Prairie falcons and peregrine falcons lift off from sheer cliffs and soar up into the clear desert air. Eleven other species are there, too, from small kestrels to great horned owls.

The Snake River was officially recognized as a natural area by the Interior Department in 1971. The Nature Conservancy, a private organization, helped to purchase the surrounding land. The area is 31,000 acres and extends for 33 miles along the river. The only people who are officially encouraged to go there are researchers from colleges and universities who are studying the best ways to manage wildlife habitats. Some have set up artificial nesting towers for raptors and have watched to see the results.

Until recently there was only one female peregrine falcon in the Birds of Prey Natural Area. More have now been successfully reintroduced into the area by a technique called *cross-fostering*. First, an ornithologist—possibly a falconer, probably a mountain climber—

Here, a wildlife biologist bands a baby golden eagle, not endangered, but not nearly as plentiful as it once was.

transfers the prairie falcon young into other nests, where they are usually accepted. (There are plenty of prairie falcon nests at Snake River for this foster-parenting plan.) Then young peregrines are placed in the now-empty nest of prairie falcon parents. This method of nest switching sounds complicated, but it works. Several young peregrines have fledged using this technique.

Rosalie Edge, a True Raptor Lover

Rosalie Edge was not a falconer, nor was she officially an ornithologist. She just loved hawks, and she was perhaps one of the earliest people in America to do something to stop the slaughter by hunters of so many birds of prey. Her name will always be associated with a place called Hawk Mountain in Pennsylvania. Thanks to her work, thousands of raptor lovers gather each year to watch the migration flight of hawks, eagles, and even an occasional peregrine.

Hawk Mountain was not always a haven for migratory raptors; it was once notorious as a site for the "sport" of hawk shooting. Around the turn of the century, and well into the 1930s, hawks were shot down as fast as hunters could reload their guns. One man reported that he shot over two hundred birds in a single day. To the hunters watching that sky filled with hawks, it seemed perfectly sensible. Weren't there *plenty* of hawks up there? But when they saw thousands of birds in a migratory flight path, they might have been seeing an entire population of a single species.

Mrs. Edge began her campaign against this slaughter in 1932. Two years later she purchased 1,300 acres of land on Hawk Mountain and established the first sanctuary for migrating birds of prey. A husband-and-wife team, Maurice and Irma Brown, was hired as the first curators. (Although Maurice was hired as curator, his wife also served unofficially.) Their job was to educate the public about this radical change on Hawk Mountain. There would be no more shooting, but anyone was welcome to come and watch the show.

That show still goes on every fall as the hawks migrate along the Kittatinny Ridge of the Appalachians, part of a system of ridges that stretches from southeastern New York clear down to Alabama. The best vantage point along the ridge is on Hawk Mountain. Every year thousands of people arrive to watch what has been called the greatest aerial ballet in the bird world—hundreds of hawks spiraling higher and higher in the sky, catching rising currents of air called *thermals*, on which they can soar for miles, only rarely flapping their wings. If you're keeping a bird list you might be able to add goshawks, sharp-shins, Cooper's, red tails, red shoulders, marsh hawks, ospreys, kestrels, bald eagles, golden eagles, and peregrines. And it all began with the efforts of one woman.

She Baby-sits for Bald Eagles

Ironically, the bald eagle, our national bird, is the only eagle that is officially listed as endangered on our national list. The scientists at Cornell's Laboratory of Ornithology have done research with

An electrocuted bald eagle, shown in this photograph that won honorable mention in a national photo contest, points clearly to one of the reasons why our national bird is on the endangered list.

eagles, too. First they tried golden eagles, using somewhat the same methods they used with peregrines. Then in 1974 they tried these techniques with bald eagles.

A key goal of the program was to try to reintroduce bald eagles into parts of the eastern United States where they had almost totally disappeared. Montezuma National Wildlife Refuge in New York was the site selected for this first attempt. In 1976, a pair of young eagles, a male and a female, were taken from the nests of wild eagles in Wisconsin. The plan was to hack them (train them to go wild) from a wooden tower thirty-five feet up in the air. The tower had been specially constructed in a cattail marsh area of the refuge where eagles had once nested, before DDT.

Tina Milburn, a graduate student at Cornell, became the guardian for these eagles. She spent most of her waking hours that summer behind a blind, where she tossed food to the eagles, careful to be an invisible parent, for the eagles had to be kept from imprinting on her, and she took their pictures. Tina recorded on film the step-by-step progress of the eagles' development. By mid-October the two eagles had not only survived and fledged successfully, but had flown out of the Montezuma refuge. The question was, would they return?

In mid-August 1977 the male came back, its yellow wing marker intact after nearly a year. But no one saw the female in that area of New York until the fall of 1979. It isn't hard to imagine how Tina Milburn must have felt when New York State wildlife workers spotted both eagles together at a small lake near Watertown and reported their find to Cornell. The pair have remained together, and though they are young they have begun nesting. The eggs laid during the 1980 season hatched, and the young were fledged—a remarkable achievement for a young pair of eagles *and* for their dedicated baby-sitter.

SHE'S NOT JUST INTERESTED IN EAGLES

Tina, who calls herself an endangered-species biologist, received her master's degree from Cornell after completing her eagle research. She is now working for the U.S. Fish and Wildlife Service trying to determine whether the loggerhead shrike has declined seriously enough to be placed on our endangered list. Looking back on her experiences as a bald eagle baby-sitter, Tina says, "At times the work was very boring since eagles, like most predators, are inactive much of the time. But those few instances when they did something for the first time as they were growing up and learning to care for themselves made the long hours of waiting all worthwhile. It's a terrific feeling to watch an eagle fly, anyway. But when it's an eagle that you fed and took care of and worried about for eight weeks, it's even more incredible."

Chapter Nine
OF EGGS AND CHICKS AND DANCING WITH WHOOPERS

THE FUNNIEST BIRD IS THE WHOOPER

IF THERE IS A BIRD that somehow seems funny to people today, that bird is more likely to be the whooping crane than the pelican or that clown of the Pacific, the red-footed booby. What's so funny about whoopers? Maybe it's the sounds they make in those marshes and tidal flats where they live. Even two or three of them can make an incredible racket. Do they whoop? Indeed they do. One woman who used to hear whoopers on her uncle's farm during the migratory season described it like this: "It was weird! Even half a mile away they sounded like cows bellowing to be milked—but still, like a honk, too, and it rose at the end in a long *oo-oo-oo* sound."

Some people also find something comical about the way whoopers look. Like all cranes—and whoopers are among the largest of the Gruidae family, five feet tall and up to twenty pounds—their long, stiltlike legs give them a slightly peculiar, strutting walk. Funny or not, this bird is seriously endangered, its count right now probably no more than 113 wild birds.

It has taken forty years of human effort to build up the whooping crane population to this number. In 1938, when research first began, there were only fourteen or fifteen birds. Efforts to save them have been nearly superhuman. Nevertheless, we do smile when we think about the whooper and all the antics of the people trying to get whoopers to lay eggs. We smile and we cheer at the same time, because crane experts, sometimes called *gruidologists*, are actually getting results.

Who can doubt that such a magnificent bird as the whooping crane is worth every effort we've made to save it?

Here is the way George Archibald, possibly the world's best-known gruidologist and director of the International Crane Foundation (ICF) of Baraboo, Wisconsin, describes his latest efforts to get Tex, his female whooper, to produce a fertile egg: "She bows, and you bow. She jumps up—you jump up. She runs, and you run. You stroke her back—" Archibald shrugs and grins. "You lose your pride pretty fast in this business." But it is worth it, because sometime—maybe, just maybe—Tex is going to hatch that egg.

Tex wouldn't dance with Tony, the only male whooping crane at the International Crane Foundation, because Tex is apparently imprinted on people. And she is very particular. She will dance occasionally with Kerry Hoffman, another of the crane experts at ICF, but she has rejected many substitutes for George Archibald. This information comes from Joan Fordham, the foundation's administrator, who adds, "Naturally she would refuse to dance with me, as she hates women." Joan, however, cares for cranes as much as the rest of the staff does. It's just not part of her job to dance.

The people at Patuxent Wildlife Research Center in Laurel, Maryland (one of the main research facilities of the U.S. Fish and Wildlife Service), once had a somewhat similar problem with a pair of their whooping cranes. They found that two females had imprinted on each other, and once they form such pairings they usually stay bonded for life. In this case, when the crane who had assumed her natural female role danced, then settled down to lay, she still had some chance of laying a fertile egg. Thanks to the wonders of artificial insemination, this was possible even though her partner was another female. If you were wondering, that is also the only way Tex will ever hatch a fertile egg. Every egg that is fertile can mean one more crane added to the population of whoopers in the world.

It isn't exactly easy to practice artificial insemination on a whooping crane. A few years ago, the crane experts tried another technique. When the bulging cloaca told them the female was ready to mate and she started to perform her stylized dance routine, they watched, but nothing happened. Finally the experts stepped in, one grasped the male, one the female. They managed to maneuver the cloacas into an approximation of the mating position and began massaging the male's thighs. Perhaps it was just that the female preferred privacy or wanted to do such things on her own, but no eggs were laid or hatched from this clumsy effort.

Next, the crane experts tried massaging the male's thighs and manipulating the cloacal structure, collecting the ejaculated sperm in test tubes. The sperm was then diluted and injected into the female's cloaca several times.

This technique got better results than forced matings. If necessary, the sperm could be frozen for future use. Of course, there are no test-tube baby cranes (no real test-tube baby anythings, actually —only test-tube fertilization methods). All new cranes come out of eggs just like any other baby chick, but frozen sperm and artificial insemination are used fairly often now.

Ernie Kuyt—He Borrows Eggs to Save Whoopers

The helicopter hovers over the marshland at Wood Buffalo National Park, way up north in Canada. It lands and one man scrambles out. Using a stick for support, he sloshes through the cold, muddy water. Cautiously he moves toward a whooper's nest—the adult birds have already flown from the site at the copter's approach. Ernie Kuyt picks up one of the beautiful buff-and-olive-colored eggs with brown and purplish blotches and slips it into a warm woolen sock. The helicopter touches down near several different nest sites before it finally leaves the area, carrying a precious cargo of six or seven eggs now bedded down in a special suitcase warmed with hot-water bottles.

Ernie Kuyt, who is a biologist with the Canadian Wildlife Service, insists upon one thing when describing his work: He does *not* steal eggs, he only borrows them. Nobody could be more concerned over those eggs, except the adult cranes themselves. He knows something else about those eggs. While the whooping cranes at Wood Buffalo National Park regularly lay two eggs in their breeding grounds, the second egg almost never hatches. If it does hatch, the second chick does not make it to maturity.

This hatch failure may be because Wood Buffalo National Park is at the extreme northern end of the whooping crane's natural breeding range, and the conditions there are simply too tough, with not enough food, for the whooper parents to raise two young. The former breeding range to the south of Wood Buffalo has been almost completely converted to the growing of wheat—a good example of the loss of bird habitat by human activity.

As a further precaution to be sure nothing goes wrong, Ernie Kuyt and his fellow biologists insist that the egg operation be done in two different trips back to nearby Fort Smith, Canada. (Think about that. Their chief concern in case of an airplane crash is that not all the *eggs* be lost.) After both of the egg shipments have been placed safely in an electric incubator at Fort Smith, Ernie Kuyt is flown over the area again, this time in a high-altitude airplane. He wants to check to be sure the adult cranes have all returned to their nests.

Those eggs have one more trip to make, however. This time they are flown, in their incubator units, to Patuxent Wildlife Research Center in Laurel, Maryland. Such egg operations have been going on for several years now, since June 1967. The whoopers produced from those eggs have hatched, grown, and produced eggs of their own. In 1979, two second-generation whooper eggs (produced at Patuxent) were successfully hatched—in the wild—at Grays Lake National Wildlife Refuge in Idaho. Grays Lake's egg-hatching operation is a very interesting one, too.

Foster Parents for Whoopers

Way back in 1956 another idea was hatched to save whoopers. Fred G. Bard, a Canadian who is director of the Saskatchewan Museum of Natural History, suggested that the only way to save whoopers was to use greater sandhill cranes as foster parents. The two species of cranes have several things in common: They both migrate, their eggs look alike, and their eggs have similar incubation periods. Most important, the chicks look nearly identical and eat similar foods.

But the idea of switching eggs was not tried until 1975, after several things were considered. Dr. Rod Drewien, project leader of the Cooperative Wildlife Research Unit at the University of Idaho, had worked for a number of years with the greater sandhill cranes at Grays Lake National Wildlife Refuge. Cautiously, in 1970, he began testing the sandhills to be sure they would not abandon their nests if eggs were switched or removed.

Another factor that needed to be determined was which pairs of sandhills nesting at Grays Lake regularly migrated to Bosque del Apache National Wildlife Refuge in New Mexico. Some whooper pairs migrated farther down into Mexico and could not be protected as well as the ones that stayed within the continental United States. Fortunately, Kuyt was able to discover which pairs of whoopers were right for this experiment.

Ernie Kuyt was eager to begin work on this joint effort between the United States and Canada to save the whooping crane. Imagine how excited he and Dr. Drewien felt flying that first shipment of eggs all the way from Wood Buffalo National Park. After leading Kuyt into the sandhill cranes' nesting grounds, Dr. Drewien took photos as Ernie gently placed whooper eggs into sandhill nests and removed the sandhills' eggs for distribution to other sandhill nests.

Dr. Drewien must have had an even greater thrill two months later when he returned to band the young whoopers, now grown

This two-month-old whooping crane is one of those hatched from Ernie Kuyt's borrowed eggs. After being netted by Fish and Wildlife personnel, with a technique perfected on sandhills by Rod Drewien, this usually aggressive whooper seems quite calm.

almost as large as their foster parents. Nine of the original fourteen eggs hatched, and the chicks survived long enough to be banded. Some even tried to chase Drewien away, flapping their untried wings and hissing loudly. But life is tough for whoopers, and for sandhills, too. Four whoopers were destroyed by predators before the remaining five were able to take off with their sandhill foster parents and migrate south to the Bosque del Apache National Wildlife Refuge. (The effort made to protect these whoopers from careless hunters has already been described in chapter three.)

What these crane experts have been trying to do is to build up a second flock of wild whooping cranes to minimize any future ecological disasters. The original flock of whoopers flies back and forth between Wood Buffalo National Park and the Aransas National Wildlife Refuge close to the Gulf of Mexico in Texas. That's a trip of 2,500 miles! The greater sandhills, with their foster flock of whoopers, travel only about eight hundred miles each time they migrate. The question still to be answered is this: Will the whoopers establish a separate flock when they reach sexual maturity? It seems natural to expect that they will. After all, cowbirds mate with cowbirds even though they are raised by Kirtland's warblers. So far, however, no matings have taken place, and we'll just have to wait and see.

The Word from Aransas

Meanwhile, there are some encouraging words from the Aransas Wildlife Refuge. The flock is increasing slowly year by year. In the fall of 1978 sixty-eight adult whoopers were counted, and six young. In 1979 there were seventy adults and six young. Further good news is that the Mexican oil spill at the offshore drilling site called Ixtoc 1 did no damage to the ecosystem in Aransas. There *are* some American oil companies with producing wells in the surrounding bays not far from Aransas, but everything possible is being done to guard against any oil spills. Only high-quality hardware and equipment are used. There is a computerized monitoring system that would automatically shut down the line and alert personnel to come running if any signs of trouble are detected. The companies also keep around a lot of cleanup and containment gear for quick emergency use. The people at the Aransas Wildlife Refuge feel comfortable with this arrangement, realizing how badly America needs oil.

Years of Service to Save America's Wildlife

There is one man who, like a concerned mother hen, has hovered over many of these endangered bird programs. Dr. Ray Erickson retired from Patuxent Wildlife Research Center in March 1980, but the endangered species research program was his idea. This finally included research at Patuxent and several field stations around the country, but getting things started wasn't easy. The program began with two thousand dollars that Ray Erickson had begged from the National Wildlife Refuge Division. By 1963 there was money enough to hire the first full-time biologist. Finally, Congress appropriated $350,000 and the whooping crane project was moved to Patuxent, with Ray Erickson given control of the project.

It was Ray Erickson's brilliant idea to use a non-endangered species as a "stand-in" to test the experimental research and captive-breeding techniques before trying them on endangered species. Thus, the greater sandhill crane was used as a stand-in for the whooping crane. Now the black vulture, the turkey vulture, and the Andean condor are being used as stand-ins for the endangered California condor.

Nobody can predict what changes may happen at Patuxent, or its network of ten field stations scattered around the country, in the years to come. Change is a way of life with government agencies. Yet whatever does happen, we should not forget the work of Ray Erickson. This quiet, soft-spoken, but very determined birdman served the United States Fish and Wildlife Service for over thirty years. He brought the plight of the whooping crane to public attention, along with the whole problem of our endangered species.

The Crane Problem Is an International One

We have already seen how the fight to save whoopers involved cooperation between Canada and the United States. Canada has given us more than one man who cares about cranes. George Archibald was born in Nova Scotia, Canada, but got his doctorate at Cornell University in New York. He has spent a lot of time at Patuxent Wildlife Research Center, and Dr. Ray Erickson is on Archibald's International Crane Foundation's board of directors. George Archibald is a true crane lover. He has spent so much time with these birds that he has helped to discover an accurate way of finding out the sex of a crane just by listening to its call and watching its courtship behavior.

A visit to the International Crane Foundation at Baraboo, Wisconsin, would be a great experience, not just for a gruidologist but for any true bird lover. Tours can be arranged if you write or call in advance for an appointment. The thing that makes this place different is that it is truly international in nature. There are over 128 cranes there, representing 14 of the 15 different species of cranes. In fact, there are more species of cranes in Baraboo than in any other place in the world. Some of the foundation's accomplishments include a cooperative effort with Russia to transport Siberian crane

Are these cranes starting their stylized dance? The experts have reason to hope so. (In the foreground is an immature whooping crane.)

eggs by air from the breeding grounds in northern Russia to Baraboo, where they have been successfully hatched. The foundation accomplished breeding of the first hooded cranes and Eastern Sarus cranes in captivity, and is justifiably proud of the new ways it has developed for hatching eggs at Baraboo—and making cranes lay *more* eggs as well.

George Archibald believes that crane saving must be an international effort. Most cranes have long migration routes, and some may fly over several countries before they reach their destinations. The Japanese are especially interested in the work at Baraboo, for the red-crowned crane is considered a national treasure in Japan. Other Oriental countries are willing to cooperate with Archibald's efforts, too. He has been to Korea to observe cranes in the demilitarized zone there, and a visit to China gave him a chance to observe the rare black-necked crane, which may be more endangered than our own whooping crane. At least seven species of cranes all over the world face the possibility of extinction. It's not surprising, therefore, that Archibald feels that efforts to save cranes must be worldwide. Cranes have been around on this earth for over sixty million years, and if George Archibald has his way they will be around for quite a while longer.

From Horse Farm to Crane Hatchery

Unlike George Archibald, Ron Sauey is a native Wisconsinite. He lived in Baraboo and was attending Cornell, that gathering place for bird enthusiasts, when he met George Archibald. Joan Fordham of the International Crane Foundation explains the results of that meeting like this: "Ron's father, Norman Sauey, Senior, had raised horses on his farm in Baraboo, but was in the process of moving them to Florida. George had been loaned several cranes for his research, and had had good success in breeding them. George wanted to be able to continue breeding the birds and not simply return them at the finish of his doctoral research. The idea of a crane captive-breeding center was born with the base being the newly vacated horse ranch. We were incorporated as a non-profit agency in 1973, and have been growing ever since."

The foundation has now purchased 160 acres of rolling farmland about 5 miles from the horse farm location. The foundation plans to move its facilities there within the next several years, and hopes to set aside acreage to reconstruct a patch of native prairie land. Like most groups engaged in serious work to protect our birds, the ICF is determined to make the effort to protect our environment as well.

Some Birds Like Wet Feathers

To illustrate the work of the ICF, let's look at another crane. The brolga is a native Australian crane. Its name comes from a native word describing its mating ritual, which looks much like our own whooping crane's dance. A pair of these rare birds, named Olga and Willie, were imported to the International Crane Foundation for breeding over five years ago. But Olga did not lay a single egg.

As it turns out, some cranes are not tied to the same warm-weather—cold-weather cycle that influences whoopers or Siberians. Instead, their mating activity is stimulated with the onset of the rainy season in Australia. There, the birds begin breeding when the monsoons begin. So Archibald decided to provide Olga and Willie with simulated monsoon conditions. He sprayed them with artificial rain regularly every day for two to three hours. This went on for over a month—and it worked! Olga soon laid her first egg, which has now hatched into the first baby brolga crane ever born in the United States.

Why do those gruidologists of Baraboo do these things? Not just because they are crazy about cranes. Joan Fordham says, "The crane is a magnificent bird. It is important to protect it for its own sake. In addition, if the crane can survive in the environment, then people will probably be able to survive in that environment, too."

World Population Figures—Not Good But Climbing

Here is a close estimate, from Ernie Kuyt in Canada, on the world population of whooping cranes as of July 2, 1980.

WOOD BUFFALO NATIONAL PARK FLOCK	76–77 adults
(1 bird still on the nest with 2 eggs)	9 chicks
GRAYS LAKE AND SURROUNDING AREAS	16 juveniles
(1 chick from a Patuxent egg)	11 chicks
CAPTIVE BIRDS	26
(including Patuxent, Baraboo, and zoos)	
TOTAL ESTIMATED POPULATION	138–139 whoopers

Of these, the Wood Buffalo National Park flock is migratory—they are the same birds that are found in the winter down at Aransas Wildlife Refuge. Similarly, the group at Grays Lake in July migrates to Bosque del Apache in winter. This flock includes no adults but, as a result of egg transfers that have taken place since 1975, sixteen juveniles of various ages and eleven chicks.

In August 1980, the ICF reported the loss of Tony, its male whooping crane. Tex is now its only surviving whooping crane, and the figure of twenty-six captive birds, above, is now down to twenty-five.

Chapter Ten
THE CALIFORNIA CONDOR—ARE WE ALREADY TOO LATE?

THE CHICK THAT DIED

THE STORY HAS BEEN RECORDED ON CAMERA for the world to see. Two of the biologists from the condor research team, John Ogden and Noel Snyder, couldn't reach the nest of a condor chick in the San Rafael wilderness. The ledge was too precarious for anyone but an experienced mountain climber to reach. So Bill Lehman, one of the staff scientists of the research team, took the risk of rappelling down seventy-five feet of rocky cliff to get to that ledge. There, the thirteen-pound chick was almost too much for him to handle by himself, but Lehman had to try so that it could be weighed, measured, and checked for parasites.

It was obvious, from the first moment Lehman moved toward it, that the condor chick was disturbed by its first sight of a human face. When Lehman caught the two-month-old chick, he discovered that the bag he had planned to use for weighing it was not large enough. Lehman had to let the bird go, unload his pack, and use it instead. The bird struggled, threatened this strange intruder—its mouth gaping open several times—but the condor seemed to be healthy. It was one of two known condors hatched during 1980 in that isolated area of southern California, and, after cataloging, it would soon be released, left to the care of its parents.

The other known chick had already been weighed and measured, and found to be healthy and thriving; no ill-effects were noted at all. For this larger chick, in the San Rafael wilderness, however, it was a different story. Suddenly it became obvious that something was terribly wrong. The condor research representative, John Borneman, tells it this way: "The chick's head began to wobble—and it died within one minute."

At least one of the biologists listening in on this tragic scene from a cliff above the nest was so stunned by what had happened that he put his head in his arms and said nothing for a long while. What *had* happened? Nobody knew for certain why the chick died, but everyone was sure it would mean nothing but bad news for the research team's efforts to save the California condor. After the condor chick's collapse, Lehman and the cameraman tried desperately to revive the bird by sprinkling a few drops of water on its head. They hoped that it might be only a case of heat exhaustion, but the condor chick did not revive.

Efforts to Find Out What Happened

The bird's body was flown to the San Diego Zoo for an autopsy. The preliminary examination revealed that death was brought about by a combination of shock, respiratory collapse, and acute heart failure, with the fact that the young condor was extremely fat being a possible contributing factor. Because of this unexpected tragedy, the Federal Wildlife Permit Office held up the permits that it was about to issue, and the California Department of Fish and Game canceled authority for nest visits and revoked (at least temporarily) the permits to capture condors for radiotelemetry and captive breeding that it had issued only a month earlier. Radiotelemetry is a way of tracking birds by attaching small radio transmitters to them. This effective method had never been used with the condors, so Fish and Game officials were uneasy about using it. As for breeding in captivity, it is always a last resort for wild birds.

Observations and studies of the condor continue, but from a distance. We simply do not know as much as we need to know about this elusive bird, which experts hope to help before it is too late. The *California Condor Newsletter*, in December 1980, said, "The death of the condor chick this summer was a serious blow to us all here at the Condor Research Center. The impact of that day in the San Rafael wilderness will stay with us a long time, but it has not lessened our resolve to do the best we can for the California condor, and to continue our efforts to obtain the information we feel is critical to save the bird from extinction."

This adult condor soars over the rugged area of the condor sanctuary.

Across the Desk from a Condor Man

John Borneman, condor research representative for the program, is still hopeful about the program's chances. A visit to the research center in Ventura, California, convinces you that he and the other research team members are concerned ornithologists who care deeply about the condor, rather than tinkerers experimenting with an already-doomed species. Borneman points out fly-by areas and nesting sites on the maps that cover the wall by his desk. He offers the latest information on the research team's future plans, and a remarkable photo of the condor in flight. He took the picture himself during one of his treks into the rugged, sometimes inaccessible, areas where the condor still lives.

A questioner across the desk from John Borneman hesitates and then asks whether there is any chance for a novice bird watcher to get a glimpse of a condor in flight. Borneman nods and says, "Yes, they're still out there. You might see one if you're patient enough, and you come at the right time of the year. If I really wanted to see a condor, what I'd do is go to the Edmonston pump plant overlook during the month of October. I'd bring food—and a litter bag—with me. I'd come as early in the morning as possible and plan to stay all day."

He hands over literature telling in specific detail about the different condor observation sites. On the cover is the same picture of that soaring adult condor—the white triangle on the underside of each wing, the flight feathers like giant fingers stretching to catch an updraft. Who could possibly compare such a creature to a turkey vulture?

You know instinctively that John Borneman has had many sighting of condors in his life. "One of my biggest thrills last year," he says, "was taking Dean Amadon into the Sespe Sanctuary and pointing out a condor to him." Dean Amadon knows as much about birds of prey as any man alive. He has written several books on the subject, yet this was his first sighting of a condor, and an exciting moment for both men. Every sighting of a condor has a certain tension about it now, for the condor is one of the most endangered birds in America today.

A Dialogue of Disagreement

The highly respected condor expert, Carl Koford, had doubts about the wisdom of trying captive breeding with the condor. He also opposed any attempt to use radiotelemetry to study the movements of the birds. Among the various objections raised by those who oppose the program are charges that the use of sophisticated trapping techniques (like cannon nets or rocket nets) to capture condors could harm them, that it will be very difficult to determine the sex of the condors to be captured for the breeding program, and that mature birds that are already feeding young might be captured by accident.

To these objections, the condor research team responds that preliminary testing of the cannon net shows it to be better than the rocket net for use with the California condor, and that both the cannon net and the rocket net are safer and more efficient than earlier trapping methods might have been. They are continuing testing of these methods, however, using turkey vultures in place of condors.

If you have never seen a cannon net in operation, here is how it works: The net is placed on the ground with food as bait in the center. When the bird or birds land and begin feeding, projectiles along one side of the net are fired into the air by remote control (human observers would trigger the projectiles), lifting the net over the birds and down on the other side. The rocket net is similar, but the projectiles are heavier and have an internal propellant.

Determining the sex of a condor *is* possible today, thanks primarily to a new technique called *fiberoptic endoscopy* (more about that later on). Furthermore, the capture of condors will be so planned that no breeding condors could possibly be trapped.

Dr. Koford once voiced a theory that the single flushing of an adult condor could lead to nest desertion, even though there is no record of this ever happening. Most seriously, Koford feared that forced laying of extra eggs during the breeding season might actually shorten the total period of time during which the female condor is capable of laying eggs. But this technique, known as *double-clutching*, is used in Dr. Cade's peregrine falcon breeding program and by bird scientists working with other species, including the Andean condor (most closely related to our own California condor) with *no apparent ill-effects*.

It is true that condors are not like chickens that have been bred to lay an egg every day. Condors—both the California and Andean species—normally lay only a single egg every two years. However, one pair of Andean condors, bred in captivity at the Bronx Zoo, was encouraged to lay three eggs in a single season. This is six times the normal rate of production in nature and is very encouraging to those who want to try captive breeding of the California condor.

John Borneman has a final word about all the criticisms. "You can 'what if' the subject to death," he says. "The condor may be biologically extinct already, if we have waited too long to start the program. Considering the alternative, I still think a captive-breeding program makes sense. To delay the capture of condors while we wait for answers to *all* the questions is surely to follow the bird into extinction. We hope to get many answers within the next twenty or thirty years. In the meantime, we must start work if the species is going to be saved. To Dr. Koford's question, 'Do we want to replace wild condors for cage-bred hand-raised birds?' my answer is, 'Yes,' for we have no other choice."

New Techniques Waiting to Be Used

In the guidelines laid out by the California Fish and Game Commission, there was a provision that no more than five pairs of condors could ever be used for breeding at one time. This would have included Topatopa, the condor already captive in the Los Angeles Zoo. But *all* permits for capturing condors were revoked after the death of that condor chick. Topatopa is a mature unmated male brought in several years ago with minor injuries and is now fully recovered. Zoo specialists are still anxious to pair Topatopa with a young female not yet mature but approaching mating age, so that a bond may be established. Hopes for such a budding romance are still alive. The U.S. Fish and Wildlife Service has asked California's permission to capture just one female condor in 1981, in order to mate with Topatopa. If this happens, at least a tentative breeding program can begin.

Meanwhile, the condor recovery team has continued to observe nesting areas and feeding stations. They have been assisted in the field by many trained volunteers (ornithologists and students) in 1980. The most interesting of these observations was carried out by Dr. Eric Johnson of California Polytechnic and some of his students. On October 5, 1980, they saw fourteen condors in a single group in Kern County, a region known to be a prime feeding habitat for condors. This large count should not be interpreted as meaning that condors are increasing. It means only that more and more efforts are being made to find these elusive birds. However, many experts still believe that radioed and released birds will make it much easier to locate the total population of California condors. They think radiotelemetry will be much more effective than conventional, hands-off, observation-only methods.

The research team had hoped soon to start marking condors with wing tags and lightweight radio transmitters. Dr. Stanley Temple, an expert in the use of telemetry equipment with sandhill cranes, noted that cranes don't seem to notice the small packs fastened to their bodies, and condors aren't likely to notice them either. A condor with such a radio pack could be tracked even by light airplane, as has already happened in the case of some radioed Andean condors in the Sechura desert of Peru.

Actually, though airplanes could be used in California, what is planned is a network of receiving antennae to be erected on high peaks and fire observation towers throughout the condor range. Such a system could give a constant check on the total numbers of birds, their daily movements, and their nesting and foraging habits. But if you can't touch a bird, you can't fit it with a radio transmitter.

It's worth noting that despite cancellation of permits for this activity some interested groups are still in support of it. The American Ornithologists' Union and the Raptor Research Foundation both passed resolutions at their annual meetings in 1980 urging that the research programs continue, with radiotelemetry and captive-breeding efforts proceeding as planned.

Some Strange New Words

Another remarkable device that is being considered for studying the condor is a newly developed fiberoptic endoscope. "What on earth is that all about?" you may be asking yourself. A *fiberoptic endoscope* is a tool now used in medicine to look inside a patient—in this case a healthy condor. The biologists have used this instrument on Topatopa.

If you have ever watched some of those remarkable films on television showing the inner workings of the human body, and you wondered how they got such pictures, the answer is fiberoptics. *Laparoscopy* is the term for the examination to determine whether a bird is male or female by looking at its sex glands, and to check on the general condition of other organs. The scientist inserts a self-illuminating tiny fiber (only 2.2 millimeters in diameter, not much thicker than a coarse hair) into a minute incision in the bird's side. The tiny filament is then withdrawn and the bird is released, unharmed and not even particularly shaken by the experience. That incision is so small, it doesn't even bleed or need to be sewn shut.

Why subject a condor to such an examination? The answer is that with most animals you can determine their sex easily by looking at their sex glands, but birds are different. Their sex glands, when present, are hidden in the cloaca, and those sex glands "aren't there" most of the year. Because birds are structurally adapted for flying they have all kinds of adaptations designed to cut down on excess weight. They don't "carry around" their sex glands all year long. Rather, a complex series of chemical changes in their bodies as they approach the time of breeding causes those glands to grow large. As soon as breeding is over, the glands—gonads in a male bird and ovaries in a female—shrink down to about the size of a dried-up pea and disappear back inside the bird's body.

What Would Happen to a Captive Condor?

On the supposition that the captive-breeding program will be allowed to continue, a propagation facility is under construction on an isolated hilltop in an area that is closed to the public, but operated by the Zoological Society of San Diego as an adjunct to its well-known Wild Animal Park. It will have individual flight cages scaled up to condor size and many special features, like closed-circuit television, so that researchers can study the condors from a distance without disturbing them.

The plan is to be tried with two pairs of mature condors. It is hoped they will mate, then hatch and rear their young. All this would take years of time under close observation. The condors would have the best of care and probably would be better off than their wild brothers and sisters. There would be no danger that pesticides could interfere with reproduction, food would always be available, and there would be no environmental hazards like hunters who might try to shoot at such a magnificent target.

How Andean Condors Are Being Used

It isn't possible to use Andean condors as foster parents for California condors, for there are no spare eggs to transplant. But in two instances Andean condors have served as test birds to help their much rarer North American cousins. From Patuxent Wildlife Research Center six young condors, captive-bred and raised in huge cages, have now been flown to the rugged mountainsides of Peru. There, researchers have monitored their survival in the wild—their eating habits, their ability to integrate with wild birds, and their general adaptability to this new wilderness environment. If these

At Patuxent Wildlife Research Center, these Andean condors have been fitted with solar-powered radio transmitters, the kind that may someday be used on California condors.

birds survive and do well after being cage-bred and raised, it may then be possible to try similar methods with our California condors.

In the Bronx Zoo another even more unusual experiment is going on. Four Andean condor chicks are being fed in cages equipped with one-way glass. The trainer, Jean Ehret, uses hand puppets designed to resemble both male and female adult condors. Thus, there is no danger that these chicks will ever become imprinted on humans, for they have never seen a human face. The fledging process will be completed from cages, simulating the bird's normal habitat as closely as possible. Then they too will soon be flown to Peru and placed in a more natural mountainous setting. No one knows for sure how successful either of these methods will be, but early reports from Peru have been very encouraging.

If They Survived, Where Would They Go?

It will be years before such methods can be tried with the California condor, and the final question revolving around any program to save our condors has to do with habitat. If condors were induced to breed in captivity, and if their offspring were one day ready to be released back into the wild to breed on their own, they would still need a place to go back to. Large acreages of wilderness would have to be held in reserve as sanctuaries for that day when condors would again soar overhead, free and wild, just as Carl Koford would have wanted it.

Latest News on the Condor Chick That Didn't Die

The other known chick hatched in 1980, according to teams of observers, continues to do well. For the first several weeks after it fledged on November 7, 1980, it took a few short flights, gradually increasing its skills at soaring, banking, turning, flex-gliding, and landing. By mid-February 1981, this healthy youngster apparently had spent the night away from its nest cliff home, but it continued to be fed by its parents through the month of March. Once this bird leaves the nest area for good, however, the researchers may never be able to find out what happens to it. Whether it will survive to reproduce or be lost to any number of causes—starvation, shooting, poisoning, etc.—we may never know, for the bird cannot be wing-tagged.

A final note on the California condor—On August 7, 1981, the California Fish and Game Commission approved a permit for federal officials to capture nine condors during the coming year. Three will be retained temporarily for breeding (one to mate with Topatopa), and the other six will be released after attachment of solar-operated radiotelemetry transmitters.

Chapter Eleven
WHAT WILL THEY TRY NEXT TO SAVE OUR BIRDS?

SOME WORDS FROM AN EX-FALCONER

MIKE CORNISH used to fly falcons. Now he flies in an airplane, tracking golden eagles for science. He uses sophisticated telemetry equipment and follows the signals of radio transmitters fastened to the backs of those eagles. "We tried a helicopter—once," Mike says. "I'll never do that again. We were following this eagle, close, as she swooped downward. Then we hit the ground—I mean we really bounced! Luckily, the pilot gave it the stick and we lifted again immediately. But if the thing had tipped or smacked down just a little harder and broken those pontoons—well, it didn't happen, but right then was when we taught ourselves a lesson about telemetry tracking: *Don't try it in a helicopter!*"

Mike Cornish feels that he has learned a lot from using such advanced methods as this in his work as an eagle researcher. His graduate work at California State, Fullerton, was on relocation and reintroduction of raptors. He is a true eagle man. The fact that he was once a falconer, whose passion for birds of prey almost got him into trouble with the Fish and Game people when he was a young boy, makes him care even more about what happens to birds like the golden eagle. These eagles are not yet endangered, but they *are* losing their habitat. Golden eagles need large areas to range and look for prey. That is one of the things this use of radiotelemetry has proven.

Backpack radio transmitters, like the one on this bald eagle, are used in research at Western Illinois University, Macomb, Illinois.

More About Radiotelemetry

You probably know that eagles are not the only birds to have radio transmitters fastened to them for study these days. The eagle equipment is similar to that used by the Cornell Laboratory of Ornithology to follow the movements of young peregrines being hacked back to the wild, only there's quite a difference in size. There are at least three different companies in the United States that make radiotelemetry equipment. Barbara Cochran Mayor is the president of one company, located in Champaign, Illinois. She says, "We can fit anything from a mouse to an elephant!"—and from a thirty-gram thrush to a twelve-pound eagle, too. Another of these companies is now filling orders not only for field researchers and universities, but for high schools.

With this equipment, researchers can track the movements of birds to find out how far they range and how they use that range. It is very useful for work with migratory birds, for instance. Some

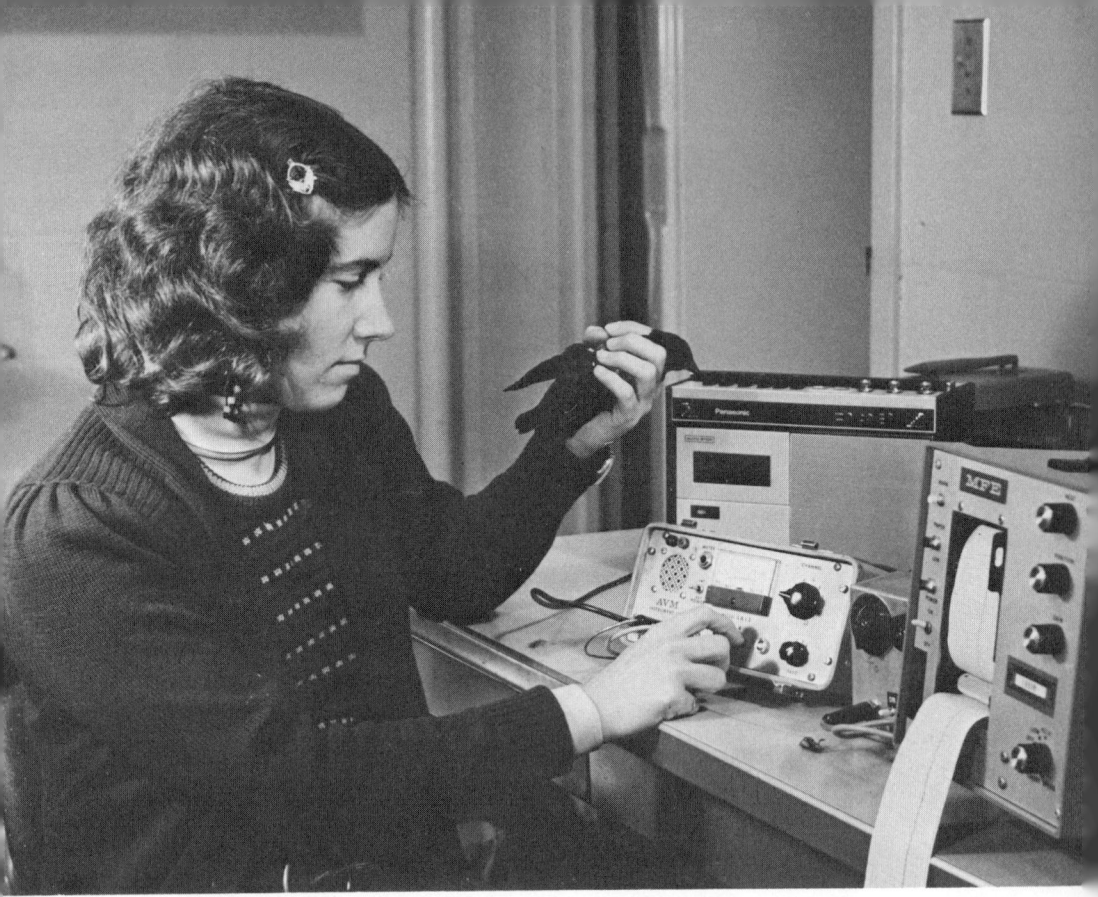

Here, Lynn Walsh Lefebvre is holding a blackbird. She and her husband, Paul, are both with the U.S. Fish and Wildlife Service in Gainesville, Florida. The equipment on the table is for tracking and recording the movements of this and other birds similarly fitted with transmitters.

people have predicted that in the future a network of automated recording devices, connected to receiving antennae, will be set up to monitor migratory paths from beginning to end.

There are limitations, however. Nobody has yet come up with a radio pack small enough to fit on a hummingbird. According to studies that estimate energy requirements of hummingbirds in flight, it is impossible for them to make long, over-water flights. Nevertheless, they do it every year. If they could be tracked, perhaps we could solve another baffling bird mystery of how they do it.

This is the peregrine falcon that was confiscated by New Jersey officials because it had been illegally killed and stuffed with its radio transmitter still attached.

ACCIDENTAL TRAPPING OF UNSUSPECTED BIRDNAPPERS

Sometimes scientists learn things from radiotelemetry that nobody ever suspected. One researcher had telemetry equipment fastened to a wild turkey. Suddenly he found he was tracking that bird right to the door of a turkey poacher who was planning to eat the research animal. The poacher got a stiff fine instead.

A similar case involved a New Jersey pigeon hunter who shot one of the Cornell peregrines with a radio transmitter on its back, only the battery was dead. The man kept the bird in a freezer for a year and then had it mounted by a taxidermist, complete with its tail-mounted radio transmitter and color band. When New Jersey officials confiscated the bird, it wasn't hard to get a conviction. An out-of-court settlement for two thousand dollars was donated to the Peregrine Fund.

Other Devices and Techniques for Peregrine Research (Egg Doctoring and Strange Hats)

The Peregrine Fund researchers are willing to do almost anything to save peregrines, but not all of their work has involved expensive equipment like radiotelemetry. Science writer David Zimmerman, who invented the term *clinical ornithology*, once suggested an idea to the Peregrine Fund for solving the problem of eggshell thinning. He thought they should coat the shells with something to make them thicker and thus keep them from breaking.

At first the peregrine experts dismissed Zimmerman's idea. Then, Bill Burnham, director of the Cornell Laboratory's facility at Fort Collins, Colorado, wanted to hatch eggs of wild peregrine falcons for his captive-breeding program. Most of the wild peregrines were still laying eggs with very thin eggshells because of DDT problems. Burnham began trying to repair the messed-up eggs so that they could hatch. In one case there was an egg with a spot where the shell was completely gone and the thin membrane was exposed. He used Elmer's glue to repair it. In another case the shell was double in thickness at one spot, and he sanded it down to normal thickness. All this took a lot of time, effort, and patience. Burnham turned over each egg by hand and hovered over them, hoping to save the lives inside, like some Florence Nightingale of the bird world. He was rewarded when some of the eggs hatched and the chicks lived.

Another researcher, Lester Boyd, is much like George Archibald of the International Crane Foundation. He doesn't mind a loss of dignity if it will help the birds. He is one of those people who has been sexually imprinted upon certain male falcons. They regard him as their potential mate, and he designed a special "mating hat" to wear during the season. This helmetlike hat has a foam-rubber crown that each peregrine perches on when it tries to mate with its trainer, and a gutter around the brim in which the semen is deposited. Thanks to Boyd's invention, the researchers can now fertilize a lot more eggs, and that's what is really important.

Now Zoos Are Helping, Too

There was a time when people who were real bird lovers almost shuddered at the thought of keeping birds captive in cages at zoos across the country. Even if they were well cared for, it seemed an unnatural way for them to live out their lives, especially larger birds like eagles and condors. But no more, because today the well-equipped, well-financed modern zoos may be the last, best hope for saving the really endangered bird populations. You already know that the San Diego Wild Animal Park was to receive the first pairs of captive California condors. The San Diego Zoo, which operates the park, is pioneering new techniques to help save endangered species. "It's a race against the clock," says Kurt Benirschke, research director at the zoo. They have what they call a "vanishing species reproduction center," where they do such things as analyzing the hormones in excrement to determine sex. New techniques include gender scans (finding out sex by internal examination), charts of ovulation cycles (finding out when the female produces eggs), hormone stimulus (forcing production of more eggs), artificial insemination, and semen and cell storage banks (saving sperm for future use).

Another facility that does an even more remarkable thing is at Front Royal, Virginia. If you have never heard of it, don't be surprised. Front Royal houses a zoo that is not a zoo, but a research and conservation center not open to the public at all. Even the scientists there try to remain out of sight of the birds and animals. This place is run by the National Zoological Park of the Smithsonian Institution. You know by now how difficult it can be to get birds to mate successfully in captivity. If some species are to survive, they must have the chance to mate, nest, and hatch their young away from the prying eyes of people. As the scientists keep discovering, nature does sometimes know best.

The Frozen Zoo and ISIS—Technology of the Future

Because of the Endangered Species Act, zoos are not allowed to sell specimens of birds. Instead, they give them away or lend them from one zoo to another. Breeding loans are not just to get a nesting where one zoo has a male bird and another zoo has a female of the same species. All this swapping keeps the genetic strain from having too many defects because of inbreeding.

Inseminating with frozen sperm is a technique that has not been used extensively with birds, but it should be noted that the Peregrine Fund has now begun a program of freezing falcon semen in cooperation with Colorado State University. They hope to be able to produce the first raptor by this method in 1981. Zoos look at this technique with interest for several reasons: Inter-zoo loans are risky, for birds have traumas—they react badly to travel; most birds cannot be easily tranquilized; and there is danger of injury during transport. But sperm banks will surely play an increasing role in the future because more eggs can be fertilized this way.

A "frozen zoo" can serve another purpose. Not only is sperm preserved, but cell samples are kept there, too, waiting for the time they may be cloned to save an all-but-extinct species. If this sounds like some far-out, futuristic piece of fiction, it isn't. There is already a frozen zoo in San Diego. While we haven't yet cloned any endangered species successfully in the United States, turkeys *have* been cloned. This is the kind of technology that modern aviculturists are already using with domestic poultry. And while a turkey is not a condor, this does begin to sound like a real possibility.

It takes money for research, a lot of it, and zoos like the one in San Diego are well budgeted, because many people visit that zoo and many others help endow it. San Diego's current budget is among the biggest in the world—$26 million a year. Yet even the San Diego Zoo would like to see the endangered laws changed slightly, so it could sell surplus animals and birds to other zoos, if necessary, to offset the costs of these new captive-breeding programs.

Connected to this work at San Diego is the work going on in Minneapolis, Minnesota. This is where ISIS comes in. Those initials stand for International Species Inventory System, a computerized inventory with sexes and bloodlines of all zoo species in most North American zoos and some European ones. Zoo officials now agree emphatically with people who are concerned about species preservation all over the world. They don't just want to see more zoo animals; they want a return of the species back to their natural habitats whenever and wherever possible. Jim Dolan, general curator of the San Diego Wild Animal Park, has said it very well, "Now zoos cooperate to save species. And yet, zoos may also become living museums where relics of birds still live because there is no natural habitat for them to return to."

And Off into Outer Space

Gerard O'Neill, a space scientist who has done a lot of futuristic thinking about some of the solutions to our world problems, has theorized on how we can solve the growing problem of habitat loss for some of our endangered birds. He'd like to see the construction of "space islands" orbiting away from the earth's atmosphere. Artificial climate controls and careful reconstruction of whole ecosystems might make these places paradise for birds that have been crowded off our own planet. Unfortunately, no one seriously thinks this can happen soon enough to save any of our currently endangered species.

The Russians, on the other hand, have already sent birds into outer space. The Soviet Union launched a satellite on September 26, 1979, to see how animals are affected by the loss of gravity. On that satellite were Japanese quail eggs in an incubator. The Russians are *not* trying to preserve species with this experiment, but trying to develop biological life-support systems. They want to see whether the eggs will hatch properly, possibly becoming a long-term food source for future manned flights that might last for years. Meanwhile, back on earth, the struggle goes on to save birds and preserve their habitats.

Chapter Twelve
YOU DON'T HAVE TO BE A PRO TO BE AN EXPERT

THEY CALL THEM "BIRD WATCHERS"

NOT EVERYONE can be a bird expert engaged in interesting work like radiotelemetry or the baby-sitting of bald eagles. But all of us who love birds can start at any time learning as much as we can about the habits of those common visitors to our own backyards. This is where the term *bird watcher* comes in, and if you've already started watching birds, don't worry if that's what some of your friends are calling you.

Because it often sounds like ridicule, many bird enthusiasts have abandoned the name bird watcher in favor of "birder," or more impressively, "field ornithologist." Australian birders, who don't mind poking fun at themselves, use the word "birdo," and somehow it fits. But whatever you call them, birders are easily recognized. They stalk through the dewy grasses in parks and meadows. They skirt around marshes and lakes or walk by the seashore. Their binoculars will be slung around their necks, unless they are raised to their eyes, their owners standing frozen, staring into a bush or a clump of trees or scanning the shoreline. They may also have a telescope on a tripod. Birders may have cameras along, but it's fairly certain they won't have guns. If there is a knapsack slung over the shoulder, it won't be for bagging game but for carrying such things as a thermos of hot coffee or cocoa, a field identification guide or two, and a bird list. It's a popular sport—even more than a sport, for bird lovers are a passionate lot. They *care* about birds and the environment in which they live. They care so much that some people who don't share that passion would say they can be a little crazy on the subject.

OBSERVATION MEANS KNOWLEDGE

Many of the people mentioned in this book started out as bird watchers; some have been bird watchers since they were children. For them, it has been a lifelong interest that has grown into real scientific study. This doesn't mean that serious bird watchers must get advanced degrees in ornithology, zoology, or any other related subject to be considered experts. It is still true today, as it always has been, that some people in the field don't seem to be interested in titles. What they are after is knowledge, the kind they can get only from close observation of nature.

There is a famous example of this in the work of Mrs. Margaret M. Nice. This woman spent more than twelve years closely observing and noting the habits of the song sparrows in her backyard. She could identify every male sparrow there by its song alone. "Each male is a unique personality," she wrote, "and when he dies these songs are lost forever." The book she wrote (in two volumes) is still considered the most accurate and complete account of the several species she observed that has ever been compiled.

No, the title of the book isn't *All You Ever Wanted to Know About Song Sparrows But Were Too Bored to Ask*. If the subject does bore you, then you'll probably never be a bird watcher. The actual title is *Studies in the Life History of the Song Sparrow*, and to the true lover of birds it is fascinating reading. Margaret Nice was ahead of her time. Born in 1884, she rebelled against being "just a housewife," and even while raising three daughters (a fourth died in childhood) and keeping house for her professor husband, she did her research. "Research is a passion with me," she said. "It drives me; it is my relentless master." Margaret Nice died at the age of ninety, and by then such famous men as Konrad Lorenz and Niko Tinbergen had recognized the importance of her work. She began her bird studies as a nine-year-old, keeping notes in her notebook, and the bird she studied first was a song sparrow.

THERE REALLY WAS A BIRDMAN OF ALCATRAZ

Another amateur who made a real contribution in the study of birds was Robert Stroud. You've probably never heard of him by that name, but he was "the Birdman of Alcatraz," and he learned about birds under the most difficult circumstances imaginable. His interest in ornithology began when he was walking—between breaks in his solitary confinement—in the prison yard at Alcatraz after a fierce rainstorm. A family of sparrows had been blown from its nest and lay helpless on the ground. Stroud picked them up, took them back to his cell, and nursed and cared for them. He even splinted one bird's broken leg with matchsticks. From that time on, he tried to learn everything he could about birds, particularly about the illnesses that attacked and killed them. Several years later, after having done all the research work in prison, he wrote a scholarly book on bird pathology.

If you have the idea that Stroud's work must have involved some very special privileges from prison officials, you couldn't be more mistaken. Stroud had to devise all his paraphernalia and instruments from the crudest equipment possible. Nobody helped, nobody cared, at least not for many years. Still, he kept on with his work, creating delicate instruments out of pieces of razor blades and other odds and ends. One microscope was finally donated to him by interested people outside the prison.

Stroud's story is an incredible one. Today most people associate the Birdman of Alcatraz with Burt Lancaster, the actor who played the fictionalized part in the movie and was nominated for an Academy Award for that role in 1962. Stroud was never released from prison, but his name should be remembered by all bird lovers.

The Case of the Mad Bird Watcher

In contrast to people like Robert Stroud and Margaret Nice, who have done very serious work in ornithology, there is the "mad" bird watcher, James Vardaman. He is good-natured about this hobby-obsession of his and doesn't seem to mind if people occasionally laugh about his antics. Newpapers across the country have printed reports concerning him. What Vardaman tried to do was to spot 700 different species of birds in a single year—1979. This would have broken the previous record set by Scott Robinson, a serious student of ornithology, who saw 657 different species in 1976.

Vardaman didn't quite reach his goal, however. On December 31, his final tally was only 698 birds. What some critics complained about was the *way* Vardaman had gone about trying to reach his goal. He happens to be a wealthy man in the lumber business, and he paid birding experts to guide him to the places where they knew the birds could be found. No one questioned Vardaman's bird list because experts had confirmed every single sighting on it. But of course, what really happened in 1979 was that Vardaman was *shown* 698 different species of birds. He didn't really identify them all himself.

Vardaman sent out, and continues to do so, newsletters to over one thousand birders around the country, telling those who see some unusually rare bird to call collect and ask for "Birdman." He even advertised in the *Miami News*, offering a hundred-dollar reward for the sighting of a blue-gray tanager, but nobody claimed the reward. Before you jump to the conclusion that Vardaman is a fraud, think about this: He has been watching birds since he was a Boy Scout nearly fifty years ago, and his newsletter makes it clear that he does know a lot about his subject. He willingly sacrificed much more than money to try for that goal.

He spent one day in a boat off Point Reyes, California, and spotted 111 species of birds. Unfortunately, Vardaman has a bad problem with seasickness. He even sailed more than six hundred miles up and down the Atlantic coast and took off by helicopter from Nantucket looking for the great skua, which he didn't find. His most rugged trip was to the island of Attu. If you're looking for it on the map, it's that tiny dot at the end of the Aleutian chain off the mainland of Alaska. On Attu he served as the "latrine orderly" for an expedition of birders. It was the only way they would let him come along.

To critics who charge he is giving birding a bad name, he answers, "Everybody has to be a nut about something. This is what I'm a nut about." And having a good sense of humor is surely a valuable thing for a birder to have.

Young People Sometimes Go for the Records, Too

People who keep track of record bird sightings are more impressed with the work of Ted Parker III. He set the bird list record in 1971 when he was a high school senior in Lancaster, Pennsylvania. He planned his strategy carefully, setting up a schedule for every spare minute in the fifty-two weekends of that year. He used the longer school vacations to take himself farther away from home. It was his knowledge of birds, however, that accounted for his always being at the right spot at the right time of year. He graduated from his school with honors, too.

Another young man, Kenn Kaufman, performed an even more impressive feat in bird lists in 1973. Kaufman began his birding career at the age of six. He dug dandelions and performed other neighborhood chores to earn the money for his first pair of binoculars at age ten. Kenn was nineteen in 1972, and ready for his try at the record. He started across the country, hitchhiking and walking to all the birding hot spots—places where birds are known to congregate in large numbers at certain times of the year. By the end of the year his count was an unofficial 675 birds.

The Ugly Side of Bird Watching

There are a few bird watchers who really should be criticized for their foolishness and carelessness. Someone once spotted a rare black rail in the vicinity of a marsh in northern California. Naturally, a party of bird watchers had to be organized to flush the bird out from its cover. The birders surrounded the spot, trampling the high grass and even poking into the bushes with a stick. When the party left, disappointed in their search, two of the more serious birders stayed behind. What they found, stomped into the marshy ground by someone's foot, was a black rail, all right. It was mangled and dying, and it never got on anybody's bird list.

Another example concerns the coppery-tailed trogon, a gorgeous bird with long, coppery tail feathers—a true tropical beauty. The only place in the United States that you'll be likely to see this bird is in Cave Creek Canyon in the mountainous area of southeastern Arizona. Richard Taylor, a young man who probably knows as much about this species of trogon as anyone in the country, does not have very kind things to say about some of the birders and photographers who come to see the rare sight of nesting coppery-tailed trogons. Some visitors come and stay in the area of the nest for so long that the parents can neither incubate the egg nor feed their young.

Trogons nest in holes, usually in tree trunks, and a pair will take turns on the nest. But if they are disturbed by too many visitors, they will abandon their nest and not return. According to Taylor, this has happened several times to the trogons of Cave Creek Canyon. "Tape recordings are the worst," he says. Male trogons have been lured away from their nests for hours by taped calls that were intended to attract the bird closer. What happens is that the male spends most of the time chasing these invisible threats to his territory, and he doesn't help with the nesting and feeding.

There are even cases of bird calls being played so loudly that they scared birds away from an entire area. You've heard the joke about the two-hundred-pound canary, haven't you? Well, if you were a bird, that wouldn't be any joke. Imagine the size the bird would have to be whose mating call sounds, to birds, like the roar of a lion.

Protecting Birds from the Birders

Rick Taylor is himself a very fine example of what a birder should be. He came to the area of Cave Creek Canyon as a worker for the U.S. Forestry Service, specializing in fire suppression. He soon discovered that his real job was to look after the visitors to the canyon, most of them bird watchers. What they wanted to see was the coppery-tailed trogon. Rick began to study and observe this rare visitor from Mexico. Finally, in 1978, he took a leave of absence from the U.S. Forestry Service, and now devotes himself entirely to the protection of trogons. He can do this thanks to the support of the Audubon Society and a few concerned individuals who have donated funds for Rick's work.

Bird-watching Dos and Don'ts

Here are some very good pointers for those who want to watch birds without doing any ecological damage to the birds or the environment in which they are found. Many of these suggestions come from Professor Beverly McIntosh, who has taught classes in field identification of birds in southern California, and who specializes in work with the western bluebird and the white-crowned sparrow. She offers some brief pointers on the subject of birding.

1. Be prepared to get up early, possibly before dawn. Birders often spend an entire day in birding, but only if they are willing to change their locations. A typical birding day

might mean first visiting a marsh to hear the dawn chorus of thousands of birds. The afternoon is quite good for shorebirds, then back again to look for the land birds out for their afternoon feeding. Some birders stay even past sundown in hopes of searching out nightbirds like the goatsuckers and owls. If you bring along lunches or snacks, obviously you will be careful not to do any littering along the way. Some birders carry plastic bags to pick up the more dangerous and unsightly trash left behind by the careless. Plastic six-pack rings and aluminum flip-tops are especially hazardous for most birds.

2. Wear practical hiking clothes and shoes. No bright colors, please. Move slowly and quietly, and speak softly or not at all unless you have to.

3. The notebook habit is a very good one, even for a beginner. Although you may not recognize most of the birds you see, and the field guides seem confusing at first, you can train yourself to observe carefully. Who knows? You might want to start your own life study one day.

4. If you use binoculars, let it be a good pair of prism binoculars. Don't buy cheap ones; it's better to do without until you can afford a decent pair, which can last a lifetime. A few of the really expert birders don't use binoculars at all. For example, Orlando Garrido, Cuba's foremost ornithologist, has trained himself to watch for special movements—tail bobbing, wing flitting, ways of flying, head movements, manner of walking or standing on the ground. Garrido almost never makes mistakes and is quicker with his identification than are those who go along with him using binoculars.

5. Do take the time to attend a class. Many are offered through schools and birding organizations, and they usually include field trips with a trained ornithologist who can point out things to watch for.

6. Don't be discouraged if it seems confusing at first. Start by listing the birds you already recognize easily, then begin making distinctions between the different kinds of sparrows, for instance. Read the bird identification guidebooks. Be familiar enough with them to know where each general class of birds can be found. This will save time in the field.

7. Remember that you are nature's guest. *Don't be an ugly birder!* Get permission before going onto private lands.

Expert birders who spotted the Baird's sandpiper, rarest of all the "peep" sandpipers, in their area could tell it from other sandpipers. Could you?

There are laws against trespassing. Try not to trample down or disturb any natural cover. Don't travel in groups larger than ten if possible.

Amateurs Can Be Experts

Roger Tory Peterson, besides being an artist, an author of bird guides and other books on birds, a nature photographer, and a dedicated birder, is very sympathetic to the work of serious amateurs out in the field. Peterson could be considered a professional with outstanding qualifications, yet he claims that he still has the outlook of an advanced amateur himself. With that kind of encouragement, there's no reason anybody should have to apologize for a lack of formal training as an ornithologist.

Take the case of John Borneman, the condor research representative. As a young man, Borneman started with a major in music education and planned a possible career in opera. He sang professionally with Fred Waring and His Pennsylvanians and even did a stint as one of the Dapper Dans of Disneyland (a barbershop quartet). During this time, he took up bird watching as a recreational hobby. "But I knew I was hooked," Borneman says, "when I was able to identify my first golden-crowned kinglet."

There is also the example of Arthur C. Bent. He was a businessman who, after his retirement, compiled most of a twenty-three-volume work, *Life Histories of North American Birds*. It became a standard reference, and though the first of these volumes was published in 1919 it is still read today by anyone who wants accurate and exciting accounts of almost any bird in America.

Those who don't share this interest in birds would be baffled by such dedication. Ask any birder. A bird in the hand? They'll take two birds in the bush any day, especially if they can get them on their bird list.

Chapter Thirteen
THE GOOSE WITH A GREEN BANDAGE—THE STORY OF BIRD BANDING

Some Mistaken Ideas

LONG BEFORE PEOPLE STARTED TRAVELING all over the world as tourists, or on scientific expeditions, the birds were flying from continent to continent, usually in the spring and fall months of the year. People didn't know this, but how could they? Nobody ever saw the great flocks of swallows, for instance, that congregated in Africa just after they had suddenly and mysteriously disappeared from their homes in Europe. Finally, after the beginning of the nineteenth century, there were enough naturalists roaming all over the world for them to begin comparing notes. Only then did they realize that many birds are migratory travelers.

Before that time, all kinds of wild theories were invented to explain why certain birds suddenly seemed to hide themselves from view. Some people actually thought they were transformed into something else, another species of bird, for instance. Others thought they hibernated, but no one ever found any hibernating birds.

This Bird Sleeps All Winter—No Matter What

There is, in fact, one bird that hibernates, and it's such an interesting case that it deserves special mention. The poorwill, a small goatsucker related to the whippoorwill, has been proved to be a truly hibernating bird. Thanks to the work of Dr. Edmund Jaeger, we now know about the wintering habits of the poorwill. Of course, the Hopi Indians knew all about the poorwill a long time ago.

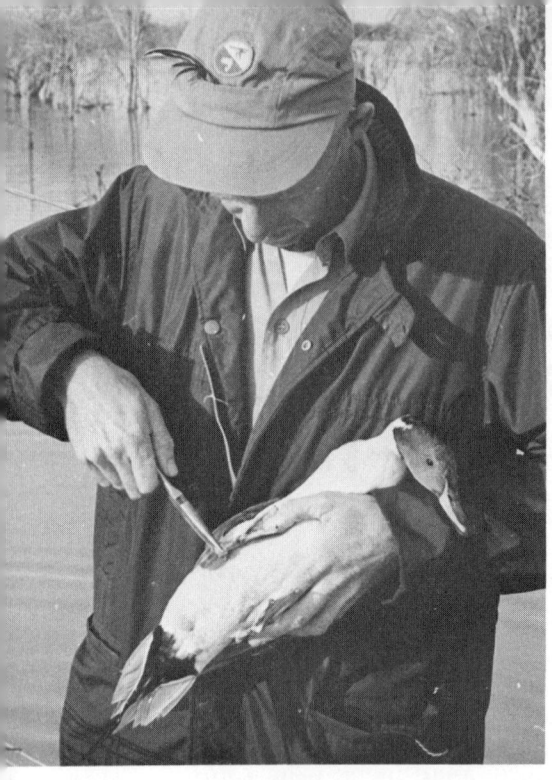

Many thousands of birds are banded in this country every year, and this duck will soon be released to continue its migratory flight.

Their name for the bird was *holchko,* which means "the sleeping one," but that didn't count as scientific proof. When Jaeger actually discovered a poorwill hibernating in a rocky crevice in a mountainous desert area near the southeastern tip of California, he took the bird out, observed it closely for almost three months, and subjected it to a number of tests without ever rousing the bird from its slumber.

Strong lights directed at the bird's eyes, rectal temperature readings, and various other scientific probings and pokings proved that the poorwill was in a deep state of hibernation. Its heartbeat was so slow that it was undetectable with a stethoscope, and its usual body temperature dropped below 66 degrees Fahrenheit (normal for birds is above 102 degrees Fahrenheit). To complete this scientific study Jaeger banded his sleeping poorwill, and the next year he found it hibernating in the same place. Again Dr. Jaeger subjected the bird to the same sort of rude examinations, yet the next year after that the poorwill still returned to its hibernating spot. It came back for four years before it finally disappeared.

The poorwill appears to be the *only* bird in the world that is a true hibernator, but the idea of bird hibernation persisted all over Europe during the Middle Ages and even up to the nineteenth century. Perhaps people assumed that if you couldn't find a bird hibernating, it was just because the birds were hibernating in a very peculiar place—on mountaintops or deep in the muck at the bottom of lakes, two of the popular theories that explained the disappearance of birds in Europe. One unnamed naturalist, as late as 1703, published a paper stating firmly that swallows flew to the moon and hibernated there during the winter months. Who knows where such ideas came from, but they certainly were not based on scientific observation. Then, the idea of bird banding was born, and at last some of the birds' secrets were discovered.

Audubon, Our First Bander

John James Audubon is the first person ever known to band a bird. He tied threads to the legs of phoebes in Pennsylvania in 1803, and the following year he knew for certain that some of these birds had come back to the same nesting spots. Almost a hundred years passed, however, before bird banding was done on a large scale. At Rossitten, in the Baltic Sea, many gulls and other birds were banded and released. When one of these birds turned up in France, people misunderstood and thought that a poor shipwrecked sailor, off a ship named *Rossitten*, had tried to send a futile message by way of a sea gull. A similar thing happened when a Bulgarian hunter shot down a spotted eagle bearing a band marked "1285." Next day, the local press had headlines telling of this astounding eagle that had lived to be over six hundred years old!

How to Get Involved in Bird Banding

If you find a banded bird, the procedure to follow is fairly simple. If the band is on a dead bird, as sometimes happens, just remove the band and send it, as directed, to Bird Band, Washington, D.C. If the bird is alive and healthy, do not remove the band. If you can get close enough to note code numbers, write those down and send them to the same address. Also take note of the bird's species, the color of the band, and whether there are any other identifying marks, like orange-dyed breast feathers, for instance.

Getting to be a bird bander yourself is a complicated process. There are over two thousand licensed bird banders in the United States, and they must have an operating permit from both the U.S.

A green band is used on this Pacific snow goose for easy field identification.

Fish and Wildlife Service and the state in which they do the banding. This is a specific permit, designating the kind of bird to be banded and the areas to be covered. Licensed banders must be at least eighteen years old. They must be recommended by three experts in the field, and they must be able to recognize *all* the birds common to that area. Furthermore, they must have a serious reason for wanting the license.

Many birds banders are scientists specializing in learning the secrets of bird migration or simply trying to learn all they can about a certain species. Bird banders may know each other well, or correspond with bird banders in other parts of the world. Wildlife recovery experts often have bird-banding licenses, too, so that when they release a bird back into the wild they will be able to tell if it returns to the same area, how long it lived after release, and how far it may have traveled. Other bird banders may even be amateur ornithologists who, from years of study and dedication, have earned their right to participate in these efforts to understand the habits of birds.

There is still much to learn about what migrant birds do on their way from one area of our world to another. Do the young birds go straight to their destination? Or do they learn from some kind of trial-and-error method the right direction to travel? Why is it that the young seem often to travel a coastal route, while the mature birds travel some distance inland? How do birds know when to travel, where to travel, and what routes to take or to avoid? So many questions remain unanswered in this most baffling of all bird mysteries. Yet, every year new information is gathered by means of bird banding.

Even if you can't qualify as a bird bander, this doesn't mean you can't help with a bird-banding operation. Thousands of volunteers have been trained (through bird societies, extension classes, college courses, and such) to assist in bird-banding efforts. And there are no age requirements here. As a volunteer you may be trained to trap, net, and handle birds, always under the watchful eye of the licensed bird bander.

A Bird in the Hand

The thrill of holding a bird in your hands gently, protectively, observing it at close range, releasing it, and then watching it soar free as you wonder whether you'll ever see or hear of it again—this is one of the very special rewards of helping to band birds. Strangely, the bird often appears to be calm and unafraid. But don't be deceived by the stare of those small, bright eyes. Bev McIntosh is a field ornithologist who works with western bluebirds and has a special fondness for the race of white-crowned sparrows that migrate from Alaska to the coastal area of southern California. She knows that the appearance of not being afraid is just a bird's defense mechanism. "Feel the way its heart is beating," she says, "and the surest sign that the bird is frightened is what we call *molt shock*. When

Young people can help in a bird-banding operation, like this boy, gently holding a duck while the licensed bander places the band on the bird.

you let the bird go, sometimes the air is literally full of feathers. This is caused by the relaxation of muscles followed by the sudden tension of springing into instant flight when it's released." Nevertheless, Bev McIntosh agrees with other bird banders that most birds are remarkable hardy creatures and are almost never harmed by the banding experience.

Out in the Field

What happens on a typical bird-banding outing? Bev McIntosh often goes out alone for her studies. "It can be both very satisfying and totally frustrating," she says. "Just try getting a net up by yourself sometime when the wind is blowing and it's so cold your hands feel stiff. If you tangle that net, it could take hours to unsnarl. And one time I accidentally scattered a whole string of bird bands onto the ground when the wire that was holding them came loose. I am accountable for every one of those bands and it took me nearly an hour to find all of them. It was maddening!

"Besides that," she continues," you have to watch out for shrikes, those little guys with sharp, pinching beaks who think they are hawks." In spite of her wry comments, it is easy to see that Bev

Caught in a mist net, this immature white-crowned sparrow is about to be banded.

Ready for release: A toss in the air and the bird will fly away unharmed.

McIntosh loves her work, and she is justly proud of her bird-bander's license.

We did see a shrike flying above the cover of shrubs where we had set up a net one day at Harbor Lake Bird Sanctuary in southern California. Bev McIntosh was concerned about shrikes not so much because they might scare away the other birds, but because of something else. If a bird gets trapped in the net and the shrike goes after it, it could be a really messy situation. The shrike would be trapped, too. It would struggle, possibly tearing up the net and injuring the other bird. Then somebody would have to go in with his or her hands to try to remove a small but very disturbed shrike before more damage is done.

The shrike may be small, but it is extremely aggressive, a predating songbird with tiny grasping feet instead of the talons nature has given the birds of prey. To compensate for his lack of talons, the shrike attacks with its beak, then impales its food on thorn bushes and barbed-wire fences. To some people, those carcasses of tiny birds, mice, and grasshoppers give the appearance of a butcher's shop with meat hanging from hooks, thus the nickname "butcherbird."

Fortunately, the shrike kept its distance that day, and before long we had a couple of immature white-crowned sparrows and an adult caught in the fine mist net that Bev McIntosh had set up with the help of our photographer, Dana Echols. A mist net looks like the kind of netting that is still used in hairnets. As it is unwound, the net appears black and clearly visible. But in a shady spot, when the net is stretched out to its full size (fifty feet long and in four tiers, each about thirty inches wide), the net almost disappears. The posts at each end are clearly visible, although they are not an alarming sight to any bird that starts to fly between the tall, jointed metal rods. They look somewhat like a badminton set in your backyard—if you can imagine a badminton net that goes almost to the ground and appears to be made out of hair netting. Any "birdies" caught in this net are live ones.

About Those Geese with Green Bandages

There are other kinds of nets that are also used in bird banding. Cannon nets are used for trapping large flocks of ducks and geese, sometimes two hundred at a time. As explained before, this kind of

Here, cannon nets have captured birds at Blackwater National Wildlife Refuge, Cambridge, Maryland.

net is actually carried by a projectile into the air and over a flock of birds, then the banders can move in and finish their work on each bird.

This may sound cruel, but it isn't. That goose with the green bandage on its neck who inspired the title of this chapter is a snow goose, and the reason for that particular banding was because of an international incident. A few years ago the Russians decided that Americans were killing some of their snow geese. To find out what was actually happening, an effort was made to band as many snow geese as possible all around the world. The American Pacific geese got green bands (not only around the neck but on the leg), the Russian geese got red bands, the Canadians got blue, and the Atlantic flyers were given black bands. Results? They discovered that the Russian geese were not being killed by Americans, at least not that year. More importantly, we learned something about international cooperative efforts and how to organize them. This could prove to be very useful in the future, particularly in our wildlife work with Canada and Mexico.

A National Network of Banded Birds

As for the small birds that were trapped that day at Harbor Lake, some of them were put in mesh bags that zip at the top. They don't like this too well, but if you don't empty out the net quickly, other birds will stay away from it. The only information that the bird-banding center at Laurel, Maryland, requires is age, sex, location of the banding, plus the date and the code number of the bird band, which automatically tells what species the bird is and who has been assigned that particular band. Each group of bird bands comes in a package from the banding center. The size is important, carefully planned to fit each particular species. Therefore you must not lose those bands!

You can imagine why Bev McIntosh was so upset when her bands for the white-crowned sparrow accidentally spilled all over the ground. They were *her* responsibility. The banding sheet is mailed in to the bird-banding center, carefully written in digital numbers. At the center all the data is fed into a large computer system and stored for future comparison.

The Real Father of American Bird Banding

The tool used to clamp on the bird band is like a pair of pliers but it's a very special instrument devised years ago by a very special man named Arthur Fast. Fast had a farm in Laurel, Maryland, and it is not a coincidence that this is where the bird-banding center is now located. His special passion was orioles, and he sometimes followed them all the way down into Central America where they have wintering grounds. In his lifetime he banded over 22,000 birds. The banding tool he invented has posts that stick up for spreading the aluminum bands apart, and then in the pinchers there are pre-

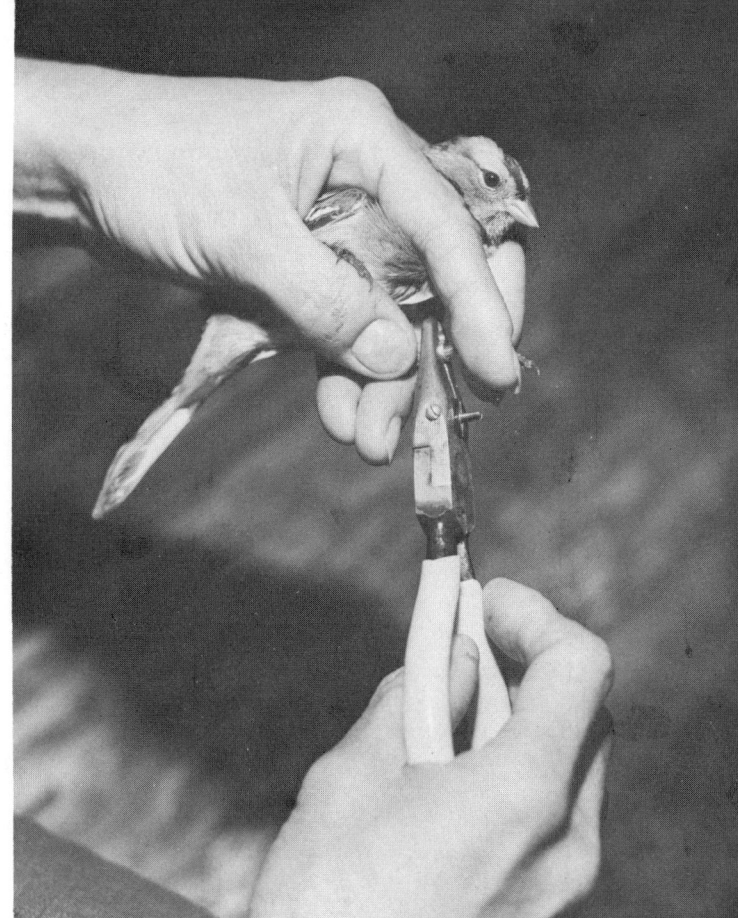

This white-crowned sparrow will wear its size 1A band for the rest of its life.

cisely calibrated slots that fit exactly the size of the bird band used. The white-crowned sparrow, for example, is a size 1A.

Some Final Data

Before our little sparrows got their bands, Bev McIntosh needed some data for her own records: the wing length, first. Actually, the length of the flight feathers is what was measured by a small metric measure with a flange at the top—like a tiny foot-measuring guide for a very small person. The bird is weighed, in grams, on a small spring scale. Bev McIntosh uses a small plastic bag, and she knows the exact weight of each bag. She checks molt condition of the feathers, and looks to see whether there is any fatty deposit left after the long migratory flight. Our birds had used up all their stored fat, which wasn't at all surprising since they had just flown all the way down from Alaska in the preceding few weeks. Ms. McIntosh some-

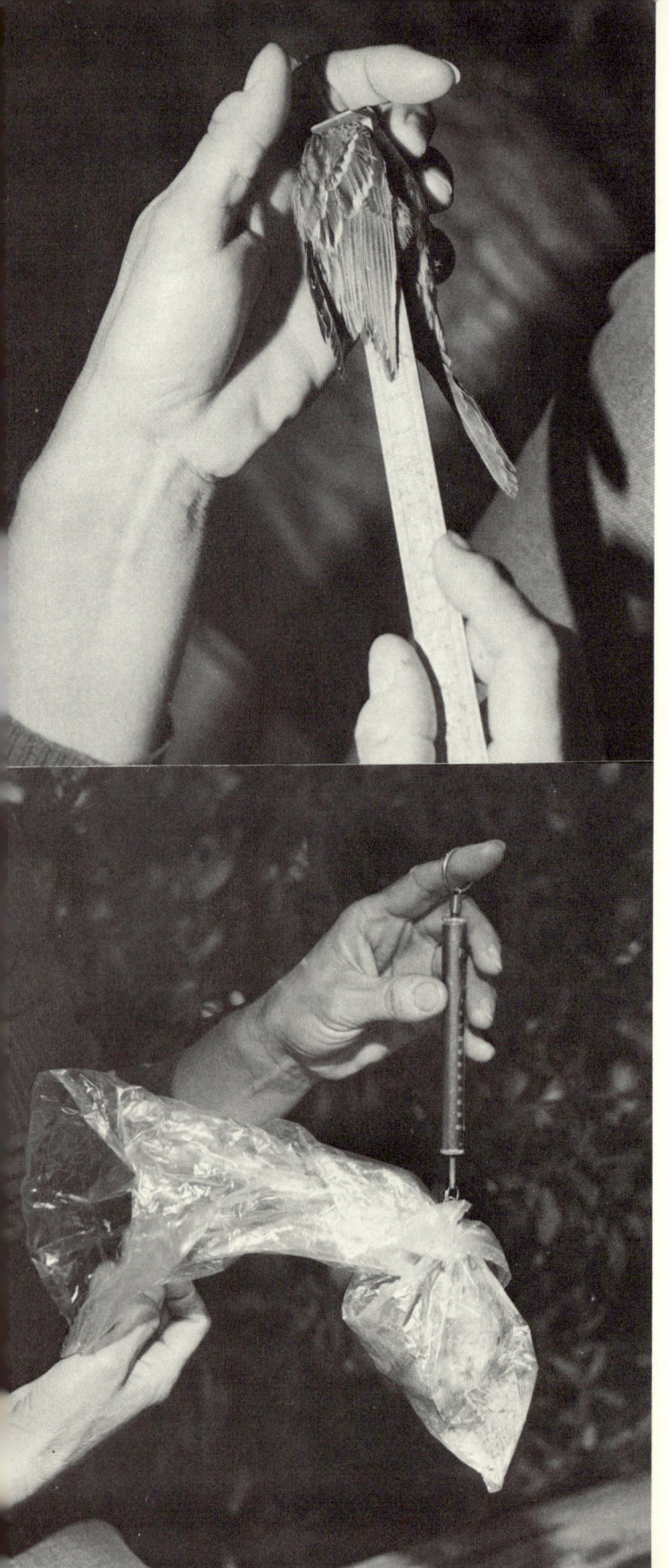

A bird bander measures the length of the bird's flight feathers for her records.

There is no danger the bird will smother — it won't be in the bag that long. Those spring scales measure weight in grams.

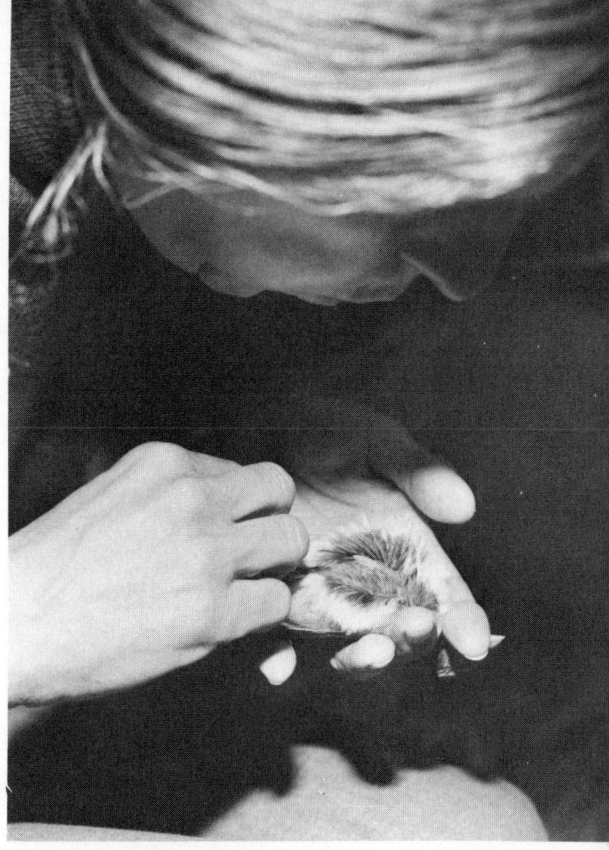

Here, the expert gently blows on the feathers to check fatty deposits under the skin at the breastbone and to see if new feathers are growing in.

times notes and records the length and color of the bill. Because she is an expert she can determine the bird's approximate age by lifting the neck feathers and examining the calcification (hardness) at the base of its skull.

When all the measuring and checking is through, the bird is released and flies away, sometimes in a flurry of loose feathers from molt shock. Bev McIntosh explains that this is a valuable defense tool, because if that shrike should happen to dive for one of the sparrows, it might get nothing but a beakful of feathers.

A Word of Caution

Never try to do bird banding on your own, not even for a science project. If you did it incorrectly, the band could be a serious hazard for the bird. Sometimes, however, bird banders welcome help from amateurs. Bev McIntosh gives lectures on her work for schoolchildren in her area, and she concludes her talks by setting up mist nets right on the playground. The children haven't caught any rare

A sure way to determine the age of each bird is to check for ossification, a hardening of the bird's skull.

birds yet, but they never fail to get one or two of those white-crowned sparrows, perhaps on its trip back from Alaska. Bev makes sure, of course, that the birds are soon on their way again, unharmed.

Chapter Fourteen
WHERE CAN BIRDS GO TO GET AWAY FROM IT ALL?

OF HUNTERS AND BIRDS

YOU MIGHT THINK that a national wildlife refuge would be one place where hunting would be absolutely forbidden, but not in America. Of our 390 wildlife refuges in every state in the union (except West Virginia, and one may be established there soon), only 41 do not allow any hunting at all. Before you start a protest march on Washington, however, you should know that the millions of duck stamps (hunting licenses) sold every year in this country have helped to pay much of the cost of our wildlife refuge system.

Duck stamps brought in a revenue of over $18 million in 1979, and the amount raised will surely grow larger in the coming years. Incidentally, at least twice that amount was raised for the refuge system by the sale of oil leases on the continental shelf. Remember those offshore drilling rigs within sight of the Aransas Wildlife Refuge, where the whooping cranes come flying in every year? They made up part of this income.

Yet somehow it doesn't seem quite fair. We create a beautiful, peaceful habitat for birds, one that is naturally attractive to each species that resides there. Then we issue licenses so hunters can shoot them out of the air as they take off or land. It seems almost cruel. Not so, say the hunters. They feel that without their efforts and financial support we might not even have a wildlife refuge system. Furthermore, they claim that more than fifty years of hunting in the refuges has actually been beneficial to the wildlife population.

These pintails have migrated north to Alaska. They will spend their winter months in the southern United States, or travel on to South America or the Caribbean.

Many of our most avid bird lovers and naturalists have been, and are, hunters. This included John James Audubon, who shot most of those specimens he later painted so vividly for all of us to enjoy. But our environment is changing, and this may call for different rules than it called for in the past. Management of our bird populations, whether endangered or not, will continue to be a serious concern for many years.

But there is one sure sign of change in all this. Today, for every hunter who comes into the refuges, there are twenty-four other people who go there for totally different reasons: hiking, bird watching, photographing, bird banding, and just pure enjoyment of nature. And the birds? They seem to be doing very well, too.

One farmer in Missouri, on land adjoining Squaw Creek Refuge, chuckled about the way city hunters bought up land around the refuge, which is one of the forty-one that doesn't allow hunting. They planted it with grains attractive to the ducks and geese that fly into the refuge, then waited outside on the perimeters hoping to bag their limits when the birds flew in for the carefully provided feast. "But what they didn't know," the farmer said, grinning, "is that those ducks wear wristwatches." They stay safely inside the refuge until after sundown (it isn't legal to hunt even in the surrounding areas *after* sundown), then they fly over to feast on the ripening grains.

How Did the Refuges Begin?

We have that pesky, wonderful, at times endangered brown pelican to thank for starting our wildlife refuge program. Down in Florida there is a tiny three-acre island known as Pelican Island, because for centuries it has been a favorite nesting spot for pelicans. A German immigrant to America, Paul Kroegel, was for years a sort of unofficial watchdog who protected the pelicans on the island.

Kroegel detested the random shooting and destruction by the vacationers in this section of Florida. He was enraged by the occasional onslaughts of the fishermen who mistakenly believed that pelicans were eating their fish. Kroegel, a small man, five foot six and 135 pounds, would stand guard on his boat with a shotgun held across his chest, warning people away from those nesting grounds. In 1901 the American Ornithologists' Union decided to hire Kroegel as a special warden to the pelicans. But they couldn't buy the island because it belonged to the U.S. government.

Fortunately for the pelicans and Kroegel, Theodore Roosevelt was President of the United States at the time. He was an ardent conservationist. Without bothering to find out whether he had the authority to do so or not, on March 14, 1903, he boldly signed his name to the document that made Pelican Island the first national wildlife refuge. Kroegel became its first game warden. (You already know about Guy Bradley, the first Audubon game warden. Kroegel was never shot at in his work, but he was certainly not popular, either.)

It wasn't just people who made life difficult for the pelicans, however. Years before they started dying from residual poisonings of DDT, the hurricanes and occasional plagues of mosquitoes would devastate the pelican populations. When pelicans moved out to surrounding islands, these islands were also added to the refuge area to protect their nesting grounds. Kroegel did what he could to help, too, though the numbers of pelicans had gone down dramatically.

THOSE BIRD HATERS AGAIN

Several years later, Kroegel had another old enemy to fight. The fishermen, during the years of World War I (1914–18), decided that pelicans were eating all their fish. They wouldn't believe the evidence proving that pelicans eat very few of the commercially caught fish. Then a terrible thing happened.

One night, a group of young boys was put ashore by their fisherman fathers, and they systematically went about clubbing to death as many pelicans as they could find. As is usually the case, nesting birds are easy prey. Kroegel wasn't there to protect his birds, and the next morning he had the sad task of killing the few pelicans that had survived, because they were too crippled and maimed ever to fly again. The boys were caught, tried, and found guilty, even though it was their fathers who should have been punished.

As for Kroegel, in 1919 the government decided it couldn't afford his services any more, so he was retired. All through his years of service, however, Kroegel was well known for his staunch defense of the pelicans. His family tells how he seldom made it through a weekend or holiday meal without having to jump up from the table, grab his gun, and rush out to stand guard over "his" pelicans. The family lived on the mainland in a tiny village named Sebastian, and Kroegel was buried there in 1948 when he died, at the age of eighty-four.

As a rescuer of pelicans, Paul Kroegel stands as a forerunner. Rosemary Collett, Dr. Joel Pasco, Dr. Ralph Schreiber, and others who still work to protect the brown pelican today must know how much they owe to this scrappy, stubborn man.

MILLIONS AND MILLIONS OF BIRDS

For every one of those 390 wildlife refuges, stories could be told of the hours of patient, dedicated service by the people who staff them. You already know something of the work going on in Aransas, Bosque del Apache, Montezuma, Brigantine, the

Bar-tailed godwits are the most conspicuous of Alaska's nesting birds, and call vociferously when danger threatens their nesting territory.

Hawaiian Islands refuge areas, and others mentioned in this book. However, there is one state with eighteen refuges important to all lovers of migratory birds; that state is Alaska.

Alaska is truly the place where birds can go to get away from it all. Bird watchers could freely choose those birds they love best from these different refuge areas. If you ever get the chance, be sure to visit the Clarence Rhode Refuge area where birds of all kinds nest in incredible numbers—estimates are over a hundred million birds each year! You'd have to take a plane to get there, but that is the usual way of getting around in this section of Alaska anyway. Birds fly there from six continents—talk about migratory travelers! Some of them come from as far away as Southeast Asia, New Zealand, and Antarctica. They can waste no time after they arrive, either. They must mate, nest, rear their young, and then fly out again before the long winter sets in. But during the months of May to September it is a bird-lover's paradise.

If seabirds are your favorites, some of the greatest seabird colonies in the world are here. The Aleutian Islands Refuge, located on

Here is a small sample of the crowded colonies of murres that populate the Aleutian Islands Refuge.

a chain of islands like those in Hawaii, could keep you busily watching almost all year round: Fulmars, petrels, cormorants, kittiwakes, murres, auklets, and puffins in huge numbers nest along steep ledges or rocky beaches, caves, and burrows.

Izembek Refuge is home for the world population of the black brant goose. Most of the population of emperor geese comes through this area, too, as well as thousands of lesser Canada geese and several different species of ducks. And take your pick of shorebirds: rock sandpipers, ruddy turnstones, semipalmated plovers, and least sandpipers as well. You will find birds here that are found nowhere else in the world, like the rock and willow ptarmigan. If you are a raptor lover you already know that gyrfalcons, peregrines,

These crested auklets, with their colorful bills and specialized head feathers, find a home among the craggy rocks of the Aleutian Islands Refuge.

and bald eagles all nest in abundant numbers in this state. Bald eagles also nest in the Admiralty Island National Monument.

If you come to Alaska, pick your time carefully, especially if you're planning a trip to the William O. Douglas Arctic Wildlife Range. No one, not even an Eskimo or an Arctic explorer, would really want to visit the Arctic range in the wintertime (temperatures of fifty below and no daylight). No birds would be there either. But the sun does not set between May 10 and August 2, and then the nighttime hours are actually best for bird watching. The area is so vast and varied, you would be strictly on your own if anything happened, but birds of many different kinds can be seen everywhere. This is outdoor camping at its most rugged. In the Arctic, however,

Black-legged kittiwakes also nest on the sea crags of the Aleutian Islands, Alaska. At other times they live almost entirely at sea, even sleeping on the water.

there are no masses of birds. They would be there, but you'd have to hunt for them.

Ironically, this wild, isolated Arctic area is also one of the most fragile and ecologically sensitive in the country. Located close to the Alaskan oil fields, this area has inspired a battle in Congress that has been called "the conservation issue of the century." There is controversy over whether to allow further oil exploration in Alaska, whether to open up the Arctic wilderness areas for oil exploration, and whether to allow logging operations in the Admiralty Island area. Alaska has been one of the few states that has really tried to plan carefully in advance about development of its resources. But some lobbying groups—oil, mining, and timber—are determined to

Alaska provides refuge for millions of waterfowl, like these goslings, every year during the breeding-nesting season.

weaken any further legislation so that they will be able to get into more wilderness areas. Exploration and development *can* take place with real regard for the environment, but Alaska belongs to the whole United States now. Everyone should pay attention to what is happening there.

A Sad Postscript—Where One Refuge Didn't Protect the Bird

So many of our refuges now provide homes and rescue programs for endangered birds that it would be impossible to list them all. Many of the birds are now starting to make comebacks, and that's

These brant geese of the Yukon Delta are temporarily caged for banding purposes.

good news. For example, the Everglade kite, once down to fewer than 50 pairs, is now up to 250 pairs, according to the 1980 census taken at the Everglade, Florida, refuge. Two things have helped the Everglade kite: Refuge workers have started providing the birds with nesting baskets in place of the more flimsy natural nests; and they have learned not to flood the area too suddenly with water, thereby flushing away those pearly snail eggs deposited on top of the leaves. This was an essential step for a bird that survives on a diet consisting almost 90 percent of those particular snails.

But in the same state of Florida, farther up and closer to the Atlantic Ocean, there is another wildlife refuge, the St. Johns River

Found mostly in Alaska, these small emperor geese may appear in our West Coast states during the winter months.

Refuge. There, a tiny sparrow is quietly dying away, and not much of anything has been done to stop it.

The dusky seaside sparrow has even more specialized habitat requirements than the Everglade kite. For the dusky seaside sparrow, getting its food wasn't a problem so much as keeping its cordgrass marshes from dying out. But nobody cared, at least not until too late. The world population of these sparrows is down to no more than six. Five are at the Florida Game and Fresh Water Fish Commission Wildlife Research Laboratory, and one was observed in the wild only a few months ago. Unfortunately, all six of these birds are males, which means there is practically no chance of survival. One possible technique is being considered: to collect and freeze semen from the male duskies for storage in a sperm bank.

This would be used later as genetic material for future techniques, such as cloning, that might still save the bird.

Most people feel, however, that the dusky seaside sparrow is already biologically extinct. We should have done something, but we didn't. As Will Post, the biologist on the recovery team finally assigned to save the dusky seaside sparrow, has said, "If they can't save a species on a wildlife refuge, they can't save anything."

Chapter Fifteen
THE CANARY IN THE COAL MINES

WATCH THAT BIRD!

COAL MINERS DON'T CARRY canaries with them into the mines any more. They have better ways of checking the air in the shafts than watching to see if the bird dies. In a way, though, we still use birds to detect dangers to our environment. When Rachel Carson sounded the warning against careless use of pesticides, people weren't very interested or sympathetic. When it dawned on them that people who ate fish, wild meats, and even carelessly sprayed fruits and vegetables, could contaminate themselves, they began to get concerned. After years of hearings and the expenditure of hundreds of thousands of dollars by environmental organizations, legislation was finally passed giving the federal government power to restrict the use of dangerous pesticides such as DDT. True, people don't lay soft-shelled eggs, but the residues from these poisons accumulate in our bodies and could endanger future generations from such things as chromosome damage.

We are now watching the uses of pesticides much more closely than we once did. New synthetic chemicals like DBCP (still being sprayed on pineapple fields in Hawaii) are now known to cause cancer in animals. In case you have wondered whether animal tests really prove anything, consider this: The federal government's Office of Technology Assessment has reported that "all substances found to cause cancer in animals have the potential for causing cancer in humans." Thus the birds and animals become a sort of early-warning system for things that can go wrong in our environment.

The Company Environmentalist

A whole new group of people has now become interested in jobs having to do with ecology and the environment as it relates to business. These people spend time doing environmental-impact studies, and they may not feel they hold just birds in their hands, for the whole web of interconnected life is their concern. Many of them are hired by business to help companies minimize the effects of environmental disasters. More importantly, companies want to know how to prevent environmental disasters from happening.

One of these "company environmentalists" is Dr. June Lindstedt-Siva. She works out of an office in a modern skyscraper, and she's employed by the Atlantic Richfield Company, one of America's larger oil companies. She says that more and more companies are now hiring environmentalists. These environmentalists attend seminars and conferences, like the oil-spill conference in 1977 in New Orleans, where they try to pool their knowledge so that they can guide companies in ways that will benefit everybody.

Dr. Siva prepares reports with technical-sounding titles, like "Oil Spill Response Planning for Biologically Sensitive Areas." It's hard for a novice to wade through a report like that, but when she explains that the whole purpose is to protect vulnerable spots *before* the spills occur by identifying them and getting help from local biologists, it begins to make sense. She knows that sometimes whole ecosystems can be destroyed by an oil spill. She wants her company to make sure that ecosystems, where drilling might occur, are protected ahead of time—and her company is listening.

Who Needs the Birds?

An often-repeated question from those who are cynical about birds is "Why do we need birds anyway?" Surely it isn't necessary to tell long stories about all the birds that have been helpful to people. An interesting clue to the answer to this question, however, comes from the early lives of many bird protectors themselves. Many of the people mentioned in this book developed a passionate interest

Dr. June Siva talks to a group of high-school teachers on Rincon Island, a specially constructed offshore oil facility that provides good habitat for marine life, including the brown pelican.

in birds by the time they were teenagers, and many of them before the age of ten.

Roger Pasquier, a bird watcher since the age of seven and now a noted author, ornithologist, and teacher on the subjects of birds and ecology, grew up in New York City. You wouldn't expect to find a habitat for a lot of birds in an urban center like New York City, would you? But there is such a place—still Pasquier's favorite haunt for bird watching—Central Park, in the heart of the city. It has attracted at least 259 species of birds, and nobody knows how many urban dwellers who need that large patch of green to remind themselves that nature still exists in this world—to study and learn from, but most of all just to enjoy.

There is no reason that any child today should ever have to say, in answer to the teacher who asks him or her to name just one bird, "I can't! I've never seen one." There are still birds to be seen everywhere. Falcons now nest on the ledges of tall buildings in East Coast cities. Terns of several different varieties walk the Pacific and Atlantic beaches, along with sandpipers and plovers. Farther up the coast, a peregrine falcon once nested in an old barrel washed ashore in San Francisco Bay. Hummingbirds feast off the rims of punch bowls at suburban patio parties and make themselves tipsy from the intoxicating nectars.

There is scarcely any place in America, no matter how smog-ridden or polluted the air, that does not have a few oases of green with birds nesting in branches. Those space islands mentioned at the end of chapter eleven won't really solve the problem for us here on earth, not until space travel becomes as commonplace as rapid transit or subways. But all young people with adventurous spirits need to develop what Rachel Carson called a "sense of wonder" about the world of which they are a part.

You don't need to know the name of every bird you see. What can be even more satisfying is to find out all you can about a particular bird that nests every year in your backyard or in a nearby park or vacant lot. Why not specialize in one species of bird, reading and learning until you actually feel you *know* that species? Nobody ever knows everything about it, but you could become an expert, and at least one bird would be a part of you for the rest of your life.

A World Without Birds

At the beginning of this book there was a story about a young man holding a bird in his hands. Suppose we lived in a world where no birds had ever existed. If you can imagine such a world, then you might have a clue about the influence of birds on human life. Isn't it possible that if people had never seen birds fly they would never have tried to fly themselves? The idea of soaring into the air by glider, or lifting into the sky by balloon, or even attempting powered flight, would have had to come literally from thin air.

So an argument could be made that if at some future time we actually do have access to the stars by longer and longer flights into space, we owe it to the fact that people have always looked up at the birds and wondered what it would be like to fly.

In a book by Isaac Asimov, *Extraterrestrial Civilizations,* he speculates about why we have had no visitors from other planets. One possibility he leaves out is that in the evolution of those other worlds out there, life forms might have remained entirely flightless. If an intelligent being never looks up and says, "Why not me? Why can't I fly into the air?" then space flight never becomes a possibility.

Those ancient ornithologists who speculated that the birds actually flew to the moon when they migrated might have been unconsciously thinking somewhat the same thing. Our envy of the birds, our attempts to copy the design of their wings, as Leonardo Da Vinci once did, has finally led us to try reaching for the stars.

The old-fashioned saying, "If God had meant people to fly, we would have been born with wings," could actually be replaced by another saying, "God must have meant us to fly, or there would never have been any birds." So we ought to treasure our birds and all living things that share our planet with us. Who knows what else they may have to teach us?

For Further Reading

There are so many books about birds available at your local library it is sometimes hard to choose. Listed below are books, articles, and pamphlets used in research for this book. All are valuable and informative. Why not start your own research project on a particular bird or on a subject related to birds? Field trips and contacts with bird experts are important, too. Perhaps one day you can become a bird expert yourself.

Bird Banding and Bird Migration

Fisher, Allan C., Jr. "Mysteries of Bird Migration," *National Geographic*, August 1979.

Lincoln, Frederick C. *Migration of Birds*. Revised by Steven R. Peterson. Circular 16, Fish and Wildlife Service, 1979.

Wiliams, Timothy, and J.M. Williams. "Oceanic Mass Migration of Land Birds with Biographical Sketches," *Scientific American*, October 1978.

Bird Care and Rehabilitation

Collett, Rosemary. *My Orphans of the Wild*. Philadelphia: J.B. Lippincott Co., 1974.

Hewett, Joan, and Richard Hewett. *Fly Away Free*. New York: Walker & Co., 1980.

Matthews, Downs. "Volunteers Rescue Injured Wildfowl," *Smithsonian*, August 1974.

Wallis, Michael. "Hunters Say Shawn Ogburn Is for the Birds," *People*, October 23, 1978.

Bird Endangerment

Graham, Frank, Jr. "Endangered Birds, Tinkering for Time," *Audubon*, November 1977.
Greenway, James. *Extinct and Vanishing Birds of the World*. New York: American Committee for Wildlife Protection, 1958.
Halliday, Tim. *Vanishing Birds*. New York: Holt, Rinehart & Winston, 1978.
McClung, Robert. *America's Endangered Birds*. New York: William Morrow & Co., 1979.
Zimmerman, David. *To Save a Bird in Peril*. New York: Coward, McCann & Geoghegan, 1975.

Bird Intelligence

Sisson, Robert. "Aha! It Really Works!" *National Geographic*, January 1974.
Tucker, Vance. "Energetics of Flight," *Scientific American*, May 1969.

Bird Watching

American Birds (monthly publication). All issues.
Birding (American Birding Association Bulletin) (bimonthly). All issues.
Graham, Frank, Jr. "The Case of the Ugly Birder," *Audubon*, July 1979.
Harrison, George H. *The Backyard Bird Watcher*. New York: Simon & Schuster, 1979.
Hickey, Joseph. *A Guide to Bird Watching*. New York: Dover Publications, 1975.
Peterson, Roger Tory. *The Bird Watcher's America*. New York: McGraw-Hill, 1965.

Birds (General)

Lorenz, Konrad. *King Solomon's Ring*. New York: Thomas Y. Crowell Co., 1952.
Pasquier, Roger. *Watching Birds*. Boston: Houghton Mifflin Co., 1977.
Peterson, Roger Tory. *Birds Over America*. New York: Dodd, Mead & Co., 1964.
──────. *The Birds*. New York: Time-Life Books, 1968.
Thomson, A. Landsborough, ed. *A New Dictionary of Birds*. New York: McGraw-Hill, 1964.
Welty, Joel. *The Life of Birds*. Philadelphia: W.B. Saunders Co., 1975.

Birds (Specific)

Bent, Arthur C. *Life Histories of North American Birds*. 23 vols. New York: Dover Publications, 1961-1976.

Berger, Andrew J. *Hawaiian Birdlife.* Honolulu: University of Hawaii Press, 1972.
Borneman, John. "California Condors: Forever Extinct?" *Audubon Imprint,* June–July 1979.
Brown, Leslie, and Dean Amadon. *Eagles, Hawks, and Falcons of the World.* 2 vols. New York: McGraw-Hill, 1968.
Drewien, Rod. "Teamwork Helps the Whooping Crane." *National Geographic,* May 1979.
Green, Larry. "Landlocked Noah's Ark Saves Cranes," *Los Angeles Times,* April 8, 1980.
Harwood, Michael. *The View from Hawk Mountain.* New York: Charles Scribner's Sons, 1973.
Jaeger, Edmund. "Poorwill Sleeps Away Winter," *National Geographic,* February 1953.
Kear, Janet, and Andrew J. Berger. *The Hawaiian Goose.* Vermillion, SD: Buteo Books, 1980.
Koford, Carl. *The California Condor.* New York: Dover Publications, 1966.
Nice, Margaret M. *Studies in the Life History of the Song Sparrow.* Part 1 Trans. New York: Linnaean Society, 1937.
————. *Studies in the Life History of the Song Sparrow.* Part 2 Trans. New York: Linnaean Society, 1943.
Peregrine Fund Newsletter. All issues.
Schreiber, Ralph W., and Joseph J. Cook. *Wonders of the Pelican World.* New York: Dodd, Mead & Co., 1974.
————. "Bad Days for the Brown Pelican," *National Geographic,* January 1975.
————. "The Brown Pelican: An Endangered Species?" *Bioscience,* November 1980.
Wilbur, Sanford. *The California Condor 1966-1976: Look at Its Past and Future.* Washington, DC: U.S. Government Printing Office, 1978.

New Technology for Saving Birds

Campbell, Sheldon. "Noah's Ark in Tomorrow's Zoo," *Smithsonian,* March 1978.
Chen, Edwin. "Species May Find Survival in Captivity," *Los Angeles Times,* March 20, 1980.
Temple, Stanley, ed. *Endangered Birds: Management Techniques for Preserving Threatened Species.* Madison, WI: University of Wisconsin Press, 1977.

People Who Study Birds

Gaddis, Thomas. *The Birdman of Alcatraz.* Rev. ed. Sausalito, CA: Comstock, 1979.
Graham, Frank, Jr. "The Scientist As Will and Idea," *Audubon,* May 1980. (about Margaret M. Nice)

Lehner, Urban C. "A Brash Amateur Ruffles the Feathers of Bird Watchers," *Wall Street Journal*, December 10, 1979.
Vardaman, James V. *Call Collect. Ask for Birdman.* New York: St. Martin's Press, 1980.

Radiotelemetry and Wildlife

Fisher, Jonathan. "Tuning In on Wildlife," *National Wildlife*, April, 1976.
Kanwisher, Stanley. "Monitoring Free-ranging Animals," *Technology Review*, June 1978.

Wildlife Refuges

Doyle, Robert E. "Our National Wildlife Refuges: A Chance to Grow," *National Geographic*, May 1979.
Eliot, John. "Hawaii's Far-flung Wildlife Paradise," *National Geographic*, May 1978.
Jeffery, David. "Preserving America's Last Great Wilderness," *National Geographic*, June 1975.
Laycock, George. *The Sign of the Flying Goose*. New York: Natural History Press, 1965.
Ogburn, Charlton. "Island, Prairie, Marsh, and Shore," *National Geographic*, March 1979.

Index

Note: Page numbers in italics refer to material in captions or illustrations

Admiralty Island National Monument, 141, 142
Age, determination of, 133, *134*
Airports, 27
Alaska, 139–143, *139–143*
Alcatraz, Birdman of, 113–114
Aleutian Islands, *142*
Aleutian Islands Refuge, 139–140, *140*, *141*
Allen, Robert Porter, 24
Alliance for Wildlife Rehabilitation and Education (AWARE), 38, 40
Amadon, Dean, 97
American Ornithologists' Union, 100, 137
Andean condor, 98, 100–102, *102*
Anderson, Daniel, 64
Aransas National Wildlife Refuge, 89, 93
Archibald, George, 84, 90–93
Arctic, the, 141–142
Artificial insemination, 76, 85, 108–110
Asimov, Isaac, 151
Atlantic Richfield Company, 148
Audubon, John James, 18, *123*, 136
Audubon Society, 56, 75, 117
Auk. *See* Great auk

Auklets, crested, *141*
Aviculture, 54
AWARE, 38, 40

Baird's sandpiper, *119*
Banding (banders), *8*, *79*, 121–134, *122*, *124*, *126*, *127*, *131*
Bard, Fred G., 87
Benirschke, Kurt, 109
Bent, Arthur C., 120
Berger, Andrew J., 55–56, 58
Berkner, Alice, 46–49
Birdman of Alcatraz, 113–114
Birds of Prey Natural Area, 78–79
Bird watchers (birders), 112–120, 149
Bone bank, 32
Borneman, John, 95–99, 120
Bosque Del Apache Wildlife Refuge, 25, 87, 88, 93
Boyd, Lester, 108
Bradley, Guy, 23–24
Breeding. *See* Captive breeding; Eggs
Briscoe, Dolph, 44–45
Broley, Charles, 24
Bronx Zoo, 102
Brown, Irma, 80
Brown, Maurice, 80

156

INDEX

Brown pelicans, 62–69, *67*, 137–138
Budgerigar (parakeet), 11
Burnham, Bill, 108

Cade, Tom, 72–75, 98
Calavaria, 22
California condor, 60, 90, 94–103, *96*
California Fish and Game Commission, 99, 103
Canada goose, *41*
Cannon nets, 97, 98, 128–129, *129*
Captive breeding, 109, 110
  of condors, 95, 97–103
  of nenes, 52–54, 57
  of peregrine falcons, 71–72, 75–78, 108
  of whooping cranes, 84–85, 91–93
Carson, Rachel, 24, 147, 150
Cave Creek Canyon (Arizona), 116–117
Central Park (New York City), 149–150
Cities, birds in, 14, 78
Clapper rail, light-footed, 28–29
Clarence Rhode Refuge, 139
Cloning, 110
Collett, George, 42–43
Collett, Rosemary, 37, 42–43
Color, 10, 13
Condor
  Andean, 98, 100–102, *102*
  California, 60, 90, 94–103, *96*
Condor Research Center, 95, *96*
Convention on Endangered Species of Wild Flora and Fauna, 21
Cornell University Laboratory of Ornithology, 71–72, 75–77, 80–81
Cornish, Mike, 104
Cranes, 90–92
  black-necked, 92
  brolga, 92–93
  greater sandhill, 87–90
  sandhill, 99–100
  whooping, 25–26, 83–93, *84*, *88*, *91*
Crops, 26–27

Cross-fostering, 78–79
Crosswalks, marked, 28
Crow, *26*
Cruelty, 41

DBCP, 58, 147
DDT, 24, 40, 62–68, 71
Delgado, Al, 36, 37, 43
Dickinson, Wesley, 30–31
Dodo, 22
Dolan, Jim, 110–111
Double-clutching, 98
Dowling, Bill, 14
Dowling, Helen, 14
Drewien, Rod, 87, *88*
Ducks, 12
  Laysan, 55
  Mexican, 25

Eagles, 44–45, 70
  bald, 71, 80X82, *81*, *105*, 141
  golden, 73, 79, 81, 104
  See also Raptors
Echols, Dana, 128
Edge, Rosalie, 79–80
Eggs, 10
  production of, 83–85, 93, 98
  switching, 86–89, 93
Eggshell thinning, 64, 65, 72, 108
Egret, 23, 24
Ehret, Jean, 102
Eider, common, *46*
Endangered birds, 50–52, *51*, 59–60
  globally, 60
  Hawaiian, *51*, 52–60
  See also specific species and other specific topics
Endangered Species Act, 59, 109, 110
Endrin, 62, 63, 65
Environmentalists, company, 148
Environmental pollutants, birds as detectors of, 147–148
Erickson, Ray, 89–90
Euthanasia, 34
Everglade kite, 60, 144

Falconry, 20–21, 73–75
Falcons, 77
  hooded, *21*
  peregrine, 14, 19–21, 71–79, 72, *107*, 107–108, 110
Fast, Arthur, 130
Fatty deposits, 131, *133*
Feathers, length of flight, 131, *132*
Felicidades Wildlife Foundation, Inc., 42–43
Fiberoptic endoscopy, 98, 100
Fish and Wildlife Service, United States, 48, 99
Flying, 150–151
Food chains, 62–63
Fordham, Joan, 85, 92, 93

Game wardens, 23–25
Garrido, Orlando, 118
Geese, *13*
  brant, 140, *144*
  Canada, *41*
  emperor, 140, *145*
  Hawaiian. See Nene
  snow, *124*, 129–130
Godwits, bar-tailed, *139*
Grays Lake National Wildlife Refuge, 87, 93
Great auk, 17–18
Gruidologists, 83
Gulls:
  laughing, 11
  ring-billed, *42*
  sea, 11

Habitat, 14
  loss of, 19, 52, 56, 86, 111
  marginal, 15, 28
Hacking back, 43–44, 74, 77–78, 81
Hawaii, 50–60, *51*, *53*
Hawaiian Islands National Wildlife Refuge, 55
Hawk Mountain (Pennsylvania), 80
Hawks, 43, 70, 74, 75, 80
  red-tailed, *31*, 35, 44
  See also Raptors

Heath, Linda, 40–42
Heath, Ralph, 40–42
Herons, black-crowned night, 27–28
Hibernation, 121–123
Hickey, Joseph J., 71
Hickman, Greg, 30–35, 37–38
Hoffman, Kerry, 85
Honeycreepers, 54
Hooded falcon, *21*
Hummingbirds, 106
Hunting (hunters), 24–26, 59, 73, 80, 107–108, 135–137

Illegal trade, 19–22, 34
Imprinting, 12, 36, 76, 84, 85, 108
Injured birds, 30–49, *68*
Intelligence, 11–13
International Bird Rescue Research Center (IBRRC), 46–47, 49
International Crane Foundation (ICF), 84–85, 90–92
International Species Inventory System (ISIS), 110
Izembek Refuge, 140

Jaeger, Edmund, 121–122
Johnson, Eric, 99

Kaufman, Kenn, 116
Kestrel, *44*, 74
Kittiwakes, black-legged, *142*
Knight, Richard, *38*
Koford, Carl, 97–99
Kroegel, Paul, 137, 138
Kuyt, Ernie, 86, 87, 93

Laparoscopy, 100
Laysan duck, 55
Lee, Ah Fat, 54
Lefebvre, Lynn Walsh, *106*
Lefebvre, Paul, *106*
Lehman, Bill, 94, 95
Litter, *42*
Lorenz, Konrad, 12

McIntosh, Beverly, 117, 125, 126, 128, 131, 133–134

INDEX

Marginal habitat, 15, 28
Mating hat, 108
Mayor, Barbara Cochran, 105
Meng, Heinz, 72
Mexican ducks, 25
Migration, 12–13, 80, 105–106, 121, *122*, 125, 139
Milburn, Tina, 24, 81–82
Mist net, *127*, 128
Molt shock, 125–126, 133
Montezuma National Wildlife Refuge, 81–82
Montrose Chemical Corporation, 67
Murres, *140*

National Zoological Park of the Smithsonian Institution, 109
Nature Conservancy, 78
Nene, 52–54, *53*
Nene park, 52–53
Nets, 126
  cannon, 97, 98, 128–129, *129*
  mist, *127*, 128
  rocket, 97, 98
Nice, Margaret M., 113
North Orange Regional Occupation Center, 30–35
Nuisances, 26–28

Ocean bottoms, contamination of, 65
Ogburn, J. Shawn, 45
Ogburn, Linda, 45
Ogden, John, 94
Oil spills, 45–49, *46*, *48*, 89, 148
O'Neill, Gerard, 111
Oology, 10
Ornithologists (ornithology), 10, 24, 29, 66
  field, 112
Owls, 30

Palila, 54, 56, 59
Parakeet (budgerigar), 11
Parker, Ted, III, 115–116
"Parrot Connection," 22
Pasco, Joel, 36–40, *68*

Pasquier, Roger, 149
Patuxent Wildlife Research Center, 85–87, 89, 90, 101, *102*
Pelican Island, 137
Pelicans, 36, 37, *37*, 40, 46, 61–69, *63*, *68*
  brown. *See* Brown pelicans
  white, 61–62
Peregrine falcons, 14, 19–21, 71–79, *72*, *107*, 107–108, 110
Peregrine Fund, 75–77, 108, 110
Pesticides, 24, 147
  See also DBCP; DDT; Endrin
Pests, 26–27
Peterson, Roger Tory, 23, 119
Pigeons, passenger, 18–19, 20
Pintails, *136*
Platt, Joseph, 20
Point-source contamination, 64
Poorwill, 121–122
Post, Will, 146
Powers, Dick, 37
Powers, Toddy, 36, 37

Radiotelemetry, 95, 97, 99–100, *102*, 103–108
Radio transmitters, backpack, *105*
Raptor Preservation Fund, 45
Raptor Research Foundation, 100
Raptors, 43–45, 70–82, 140–141
  See also Eagles; Falcons; Hawks
Refuges. *See* Wildlife refuges
Rehabilitation, 36–49
  See also Injured birds
Replogle, Brian, 44
Riddle, Bill, 45
Rigby, Dick, 25
Roadrunner, *33*
Road signs, 28
Rocket nets, 97, 98
Roosevelt, Theodore, 137

St. Johns River Refuge, 144–145
San Diego Wild Animal Park, 101, 109
San Diego Zoo, 109, 110

Sandpiper, Baird's, *119*
Sauey, Ron, 92
Schlemmer, Tillie Laysan, 55
Schreiber, Betty Anne, 66
Schreiber, Ralph, 65–67
Scott, Peter, 52
Sea gull, 11
Semen:
    frozen, 145
    See also Artificial insemination; Sperm
Sex, determination of, 97, 98, 100–101, 109
Shrikes, 126, 128
Sierra Club, 56
Sinkholes, 9
Siva, June, 148, *149*
Smithsonian Institution, National Zoological Park of the, 109
Smuggling, 21–22, 34
Snake River (Idaho), 78–79
Snyder, Noel, 94
Soviet Union, 111, 129–130
Space, outer, 111
Sparrows:
    dusky seaside, 145–146
    white-crowned, 125–126, *127*, 128, 131, *131*, 133, 134
Sperm, 76
    frozen, 85, 110
    See also Semen
Sperm banks, 109, 110, 145
Stool pigeon, 19
Stroud, Robert, 114
Suncoast Seabird Sanctuary, 40–42

Taylor, Richard, 116–117
Temple, Stanley, 22, 99–100

Tern, least, 14–15, *15*
Thermals, 80
Threatened birds, 59
Trade, illegal, 19–22, 34
Traffic U.S.A., 22
Trapping techniques, 97–98
    See also Nets
Trogon, coppery-tailed, 116–117
Tucker, Vance, 11

Vardaman, James, 114–115
Vision, 10, 13
Vulture, American, 12

Weight, measurement of, 131, *132*
Wetmore, Alexander, 55
Whooping cranes, 25–26, 83–93, *84, 88, 91*
Wiessinger, John, 73
Wildfowl Trust, 52
Wildlife refuges (sanctuaries), 103, 135–146
William O. Douglas Arctic Wildlife Range, 141
Williams, C. B., 21
Wilson, E. O., 10
Wilson, Scott, 57–58
Wood Buffalo National Park, 86, 87, 89, 93
Woodpecker, red-cockaded, 51–52
World Wildlife Fund, 22

Zahm, Gary, 25
Zimmerman, David, 108
Zoological Society of San Diego, 101
Zoos, 109–111